What's in a Word?

What's
in a
Word?

Etymological Gossip About Some
Interesting English Words

ROBERT GORRELL

UNIVERSITY OF NEVADA PRESS

RENO & LAS VEGAS

University of Nevada Press, Reno, Nevada 89557 USA
Copyright © 2001 by University of Nevada Press
All rights reserved
Manufactured in the United States of America
Design by Kaelin Chappell

Library of Congress Cataloging-in-Publication Data
Gorrell, Robert M.
What's in a word? : etymological gossip about some
interesting English words / Robert Gorrell.
p. cm.
Includes index.
ISBN 0-87417-367-1 (alk. paper)
1. English language—Etymology.
2. English language—Foreign elements.
3. English language—Foreign words and phrases.
I. Title.
PE1574.G67 2001
422'.4—dc21   00-011146

The paper used in this book meets the requirements of
American National Standard for Information Sciences—
Permanence of Paper for Printed Library Materials,
ANSI Z39.48-1984.
Binding materials were selected for strength and durability.

First Printing
10 09 08 07 06 05 04 03 02 01   5 4 3 2 1

CONTENTS

ACKNOWLEDGMENTS

Stephen N. Tchudi and Phillip C. Boardman read the manuscript and also the revisions and made sensible and useful suggestions; I am grateful. I am grateful also to Margaret F. Dalrymple, Julie Schorfheide, and the staff of the University of Nevada Press for careful editing and to my wife, Joie, for ideas and tolerance.

What's in a Word?

Introduction

WORDS ARE THE MOST USEFUL TOOLS THAT human beings have managed to develop. We use them for thinking, for creating, for producing, for conducting all the world's business. It is not surprising that we are also interested in words as objects, thinking not just of their utility for communication, but also of their shape, their sound, their history.

Words, for example, have long been endowed with mystical powers beyond their meaning—ability to cast spells or grant wishes—*abracadabra,* or *open sesame.* A grammarian was once a person versed in magic; the word *gramarye*, from Greek *gramma*, something written or a word, meant magic or occult knowledge and reflected superstitious beliefs in the power of words. Although word magic was most apparent in some earlier societies—where words had power to heal or kill or were so dangerous they could not be uttered—we still can censor books that use certain words or punish users of words deemed politically incorrect. I detect a kind of obscure irony in modern technology's development of bank vaults that can be opened only by spoken words.

We also use words in various kinds of play, serious and trivial. Children find words fascinating for their sounds as well as their uses and create jingles for jumping rope or counting—*eeny, meeny, miney, moe*. Our interest in words for themselves—for their shape rather than their symbolic significance—explains the popularity of games like Scrabble or television shows like *Wheel of Fortune*. Crossword puzzles rely on both our interest in the shape of words and our concern for meaning.

The most serious of the games we play with words is etymology, the study of the history of words, their origin and development. It attracts anyone interested in words and is also pursued by serious scholars versed in comparative linguistics. It is fascinating in itself, but it also is useful as a way of improving anyone's use of the language. John Ruskin, in the nineteenth century, was eloquent on the importance of "looking intensely at words." A well-educated person is "learned in the peerage of words ... remembers all their ancestry, their intermarriages, distant relationships, and the extent to which they were admitted, and offices they held, among the national noblesse of words at any time, and in any country."

This book, however, does not attempt to examine the peerage of all words; it is not an etymological dictionary. It is, rather, a kind of verbal gossip column, a look at a few family trees that seem to me interesting, sometimes because their history is unusual or obscure. The stories illustrate different ways in which words develop and become part of the English language, or sometimes ways in which they cease to be useful and disappear.

We have no information on what language was like when it began. The earliest records we have show language already in a high stage of development. Guesses that language developed as an extension of animal sounds or as imitations of sounds in nature or as more or less involuntary grunts and groans are interesting speculations that cannot be proved, although some novels about primitive people exploit them. Probably for a variety of reasons language seems to have emerged as vertebrates became human, part of the process. Language and humanity may be two aspects of the same thing; language may be a way of defining man.

In any event, it seems that as early as 3500 B.C. a language was spoken by a nomadic people who moved from Asia to various parts of what is now Europe. This language, which we now call Indo-European, was the ancestor of English and many other modern languages. It existed long before there were historical records, but it has been approximately reconstructed by scholars working with comparisons of existing languages. Notice the following table of words in several modern and ancient languages:

English	Lithuanian	Celtic	Latin	Greek	Persian	Sanskrit
three	tri	tri	tres	treis	thri	tri
seven	septyni	secht	septem	hepta	hapta	sapta
me	manen	me	me	me	me	me
mother	moter	mathair	mater	meter	matar	matar
brother	brolis	brathair	frater	phrate	—	bhratar
night	naktis	—	noctis	nuktos	—	nakta

The parallels led scholars to postulate a common parent language and to construct words that must have been in the early language to account for those in the later ones. To account for *three* and *tri* and *tres* linguists have constructed the Indo-European base *trei,* marking the word with an asterisk to indicate that it is a reconstruction. The Indo-European base for *brother* is *brater*. These are, of course, conjectural, but the reconstruction has been worked out in so much detail that its essential truth is accepted by linguists.

Nothing is known directly of the prehistoric people who spoke Indo-European, but with the language reconstructed some inferences are possible. For instance, the Indo-Europeans had words for bears, wolves, and pine trees, but not for alligators, elephants, and palm trees. They did not live in a tropical climate. They had horses, and drank their milk, but did not use them as draft animals. They hunted and fished. Most importantly, they moved about through the centuries so that their language is behind most of the languages of Europe and many important languages of Asia.

One of these languages, Celtic, was established in England by the time any historic records became available, but it was largely displaced, first by Romans and then, when the Romans left about A.D. 400, by Germanic tribes. These tribes, Angles and Saxons, conquered the Celts and withstood occasional invasions from Danes and Norwegians and established the Germanic language that we now call Anglo-Saxon or Old English. It showed some influence from the Celts and Romans but generally was the language the tribes had brought from the continent. Their language was written, and enough examples survive from the half-dozen centuries when it prevailed to provide an accurate notion of what the language was like. For example, following are the first lines of chapter 5 of the Gospel of Saint Matthew in an Anglo-Saxon version of about A.D. 1000:

> Soþlice, ða se Hælend geseh ða menigu, he astah on ðone munt; and ða he sæt, a genealæhton his leorning-cnihtas to him. And he ontyde his muþ and lærde hi and cwæð.

Following is a literal translation:

> Truly, when the Holy One saw the manyness [of people], he climbed on the mount and there he sat, then near-came his learning-knights [disciples] to him. And he opened his mouth and taught them and said.

In 1066 Norman invaders conquered England and established French as the official language of the country. It became the language of the court, of government and big business. Harold, defeated by William the Conqueror at the Battle of Hastings, was the last English king for three hundred years. The presence of the new language accel-

erated the process of borrowing, which had been characteristic of the English as they adopted words from the
Romans or the Danes. Words like *government, commerce,
education,* and *ecclesiastics* came into English from the
Normans. But most English people went on speaking
Anglo-Saxon. Meat appeared on a wealthy Norman's table
named with the Norman equivalents of our words *beef,
veal, pork, mutton,* although the common people tending
the animals that produced the meat called them by the
Anglo-Saxon equivalents of *cow, calf, swine, sheep.* In general, English has retained words of Anglo-Saxon origin
for everyday affairs—*house, man, wife, child, bed, eat,
live, die, love, fight*—but has borrowed widely for all sorts
of specialized matters. The process has continued, and in
an unabridged dictionary today a large percentage of the
words are borrowed, from many languages, more than
half of them from Latin and Greek. In any passage of
modern prose, however, as many as half the words are
likely to be native, especially words marking grammar—
a, an, the, and, but, who, that, he, it, in, on, by.

Stories about words we use today, therefore, are likely
to begin with a word in Old English or a word in Greek
or Latin. Many of these have come through modern Romance languages: music terms from Italy, *andante, piano,
concerto, piccolo*; religious terms through French, *bishop,*

mass, priest, monk. Increasingly English has borrowed from other languages; *alcohol* and *sash* from Arabic, *sauna* from Finnish, *kimono* and *sushi* from Japanese, *chaps* and *rodeo* from Mexican Spanish, *tea* and *typhoon* from Chinese, *chaparral* from Basque, *spoor* from Dutch, and so on.

A small percentage of the words in a dictionary, however, have different kinds of origins, and some of them are included in the stories in this book because of their interest. A few words have simply been coined. *Kodak* and *Frigidaire* were created as trade names; *serendipity* and *pandemonium* were literary coinages. Many words, including *America*, have been coined from proper names: *sandwich* from the Earl of Sandwich, *ampere* from André Marie Ampère, *maverick* from Samuel A. Maverick. Acronyms, increasingly popular in recent years, often function as words, and we use them without remembering what the letters stand for: USO, IRS, sometimes pronouncing them as words, NASA, WAC.

As part of a general tendency toward linguistic economy, speakers of English also make new words, especially slang words, by abbreviating old ones. Many of these become part of the standard language: *zoo* from *zoological gardens*, *bus* from *omnibus*, *piano* from *pianoforte*. Many clippings are restricted to informal usage: *exam, prof, exec, doc, curio, coke*. Some of these seem characteristic of only one variety of English and tend not to cross oceans. Australia has a number of clippings that sound almost affectionate: *footie* for *football,* *cozzie* for a bathing suit from *swimming costume,* *mozzie* for *mosquito.* British *nappy* for a diaper from *napkin,* *brolly* for an *umbrella,* *telly* for *television,* or *sussie* for a suspect in police talk are not widely used in America.

Probably the most common way currently of expanding the vocabulary is by compounding, putting two or more existing words together to create a new word. Many of the words we have borrowed, of course, have been compounded in another language. *Delicatessen* was a German combination of French *délicat,* delightful, and German *essen,* food, before it was borrowed by English. But we are constantly producing new combinations of words already in the language: *roughneck, cowboy, bulldog, pawnbroker.*

Similar to compounding is the use of affixes to create new words, sometimes nouns from verbs or verbs from nouns, sometimes entirely new words. Prefixes like *ante-,* *pre-, dis-, over-* and suffixes like *-dom, -ize, -able, -ment* produce words like *prenatal, overbearing, martyrdom.* Some prefixes have a variety of meanings: *in-* can mean in, within, into, toward, not, no, without, and may be spelled *il-, im-,* or *ir-.* Many words, some not likely to survive, have been created in recent times with faddish suffixes like

-orium, -wise, -orama, -burger. Sometimes the use of affixes is complicated by what linguists call back formation, the opposite of the usual procedure. For example, *editor,* which looks like *edit* plus a suffix, is the original word, and *edit* was formed from it. *Enthuse* is a back formation from *enthusiasm,* and as a relative newcomer it is still looked on with suspicion by some editors.

A few words have been created by a process called folk etymology, a testament to the popular interest in the origin of words. From the look of a word people fashion a notion about its origin and turn it into a new word. A well-known example is the word *shamefaced.* It developed from the earlier English word *shamefast,* which had nothing to do with the face. It combined *shame,* a synonym for *modesty,* with *fast,* meaning fixed or confirmed; *shamefast* was a complimentary term. Mishearing of the final syllable of the word changed both its spelling and its meaning. A more recent example is the popular change in English of French *chaise longue,* a long chair. Apparently assuming that *longue* is a mistake for *lounge,* American furniture stores sell *chaise lounges.* Most often folk etymology just provides a mistaken guess about a word's origin, like the notion that *sticks,* for the hinterlands, comes from the river Styx or that *gaudy* comes from the name of Spanish architect Antonio Gaudí i Cornet.

In many ways word stories are most interesting not for how a word started but for what it has become. Language is constantly changing. Borrowed words shift in meaning and shape to fit the patterns of their new language. Both native and borrowed words continue to shift as they are used, affected by the contexts in which they customarily appear. One common pattern is known linguistically as pejoration and amelioration, or less technically as degradation and elevation. That is, a word acquires less or more favorable connotations. *Boor* and *villain* started as names for a peasant and farm worker, without uncomplimentary implications. *Silly* meant happy or blest and then innocent or simple. *Cniht* was simply a name for a boy or lad, but it became *knight* and as an example of elevation came to refer to a champion in medieval romance and then a British rank. In another pattern of semantic change, words shift by generalization and specialization. *Hazard* was the name of a game of dice; it has generalized to refer to any kind of risk or jeopardy. *Arrive,* from Latin *ripa,* shore, originally applied specifically to the end of a voyage but generalized to apply to the end of any journey. On the other hand, *deer* in the sixteenth century could refer to any animal; it has specialized to refer to only one. *Starve* originally meant generally to die or perish; it specialized to mean to die from lack of food.

Words change and expand their meanings in various other ways so that a current dictionary may list a dozen or so meanings for many words. By metaphorical association we turn words to many new uses. A tap can be a faucet, a light touch, a tool for putting threads on a rod, or a place that serves liquor. A dog can be an animal, an andiron, a man as a gay dog or a lucky dog or a dirty dog, or a mechanical device. We can dog someone's footsteps or put on the dog. A foot can be the end of a leg, a base of a pedestal or the bottom of a page, the end of bed, twelve inches, or a metrical unit of verse.

What follows is a series of stories about some English words that seem to me interesting. Sometimes their ancestry is unusual, sometimes amusing; sometimes it reveals special insight into current implications of a word. I have tried to make the stories accurate, to distinguish speculation from fact.

Bibliographical Note

The information in the word stories has been collected from a number of readily available sources, and readers interested in etymology may wish to consult them. The most important source is the *Oxford English Dictionary*, the monumental work of a group of scholars published first in 1928 and revised in a second edition in 1989 in twenty volumes. Based on historical principles, the dictionary provides etymological information on each entry as well as quotations illustrating its use. The *Shorter Oxford English Dictionary* (1993) in two volumes includes virtually all the words in the twenty-volume edition, but without the extensive illustrative quotations. Modeled on the *OED* is the *Dictionary of American English*, which appeared in 1938 and was completed in four volumes in 1944. Another useful supplement to the *OED* is *A Dictionary of Americanisms on Historical Principles, 1951*. There are, of course, many other standard dictionaries that include etymological information, in America particularly *Merriam Webster's New International Dictionary*, unabridged. A dozen or more smaller desk dictionaries contain some etymological information; of those I find *Webster's New World Dictionary* the most useful, partly because it includes information on Indo-European roots. I am fond of another lesser-known dictionary even though it is long out of date, the *Century Dictionary and Cyclopedia*, completed in eight volumes in 1891, with an atlas and cyclopedia of names to follow. The *Oxford Dictionary of English Etymology* has useful information on many words.

Other earlier dictionaries are often interesting, although less readily available: Samuel Johnson's in 1755;

Thomas Sheridan's, 1789, with an interesting guide to pronunciation; and Francis Grose's often amusing *Classical Dictionary of the Vulgar Tongue*, 1796.

Various kinds of specialized dictionaries are also available—for example, *The Australian National Dictionary,* and various dialect dictionaries. Dictionaries of slang sometimes have information on the origin of expressions: Eric Partridge, *Dictionary of Slang and Unconventional English;* Harold Wentworth and Stuart Berg Flexner, *Dictionary of American Slang;* and John Ayto and John Simpson, *Oxford Dictionary of Modern Slang.*

CHAPTER 1

Roots from Rome

THE LAST ROMAN TROOPS WERE WITHDRAWN from Britain about A.D. 410, and during the next two centuries Germanic tribes from the Continent moved across the Channel. They established their language, a fusion of the dialects spoken by the various invading tribes, which is now known as Old English or Anglo-Saxon. Even before the language was transported to Britain, however, the influence of Latin had begun, as the tribesmen picked up words from the Roman armies and merchants moving through the Germanic territories.

English continued to borrow from Latin through the Old English period, from 450 to 1150, influenced by the introduction of Christianity and then most significantly by the Norman Conquest of 1066 and the establishment of Norman French as the official language. Old English prevailed but retained many words from Latin through the French; and then with the Renaissance borrowing accelerated, and Latin began accounting for more and more of the English vocabulary. As modern English developed, the language not only adopted Latin words but also used Latin words like *scribere*, to write; *sequi*, to follow; or *facere*, to do or make, as roots for thousands of English words. Latin *ducere*, to lead, is the source for *duct, dock, douche, induce, induct, reduce, seduce, conduct, educate, production*, and many others. Words in this chapter indicate some of the ways in which Latin roots have influenced English.

apron. *Apron*, like *napkin* and *map*, goes back to Latin *mappa*, a napkin or the cloth on which maps were painted, which produced Old French *nape*, tablecloth, which was adopted in Middle English to form the word *naperon*, for a different use of the cloth. Then through confusion between *a* and *an*, *a napron* became *an apron*. The same kind of blunder, called metathesis by linguists, changed *a numpire* to *an umpire* and *a nadder* to *an adder*. Reversing the process changed *an ekename* to *a nickname*. The process can be observed in more recent times in the dropping of the *a* in *another* in some nonstandard usage: "a whole nother ball game."

bevy. When Adam in Milton's *Paradise Lost* beholds a bevy of fair women, the word *bevy* has come a long way from its origin. From Latin *bibere*, to drink, and then Old French *bevee*, the word came into English as the name for a group of drinkers, and then for a group of birds or animals or people, usually women. At one stage the word became a favorite of promoters of burlesque shows, who liked in their advertising to promise a "bevy of beauties." More obviously, *bibere* is behind English *beverage*, through Old French *beivre*, and less obviously behind *bib*.

bib. Latin *bibere*, to drink, is behind *bibulous* and *imbibe*, which keep the Latin word's main meaning, but by a shift in emphasis *bibere* was also the origin of *bib*, the cloth tied around a child's neck to catch the spillover from drinking or eating. In the phrase "your best bib and tucker," *bib* combines with the name for a loose shoulder cover or collar in a nonserious expression about clothes.

captain. Latin *caput*, head, is also behind many words in English, sometimes through French. *Captain*, for example, came through Old French *capitaine*, and *corporal* through French *caporal*. *Chief* and *chieftan* come from Old French *chef*, a leader, as does *chef*, shortened from *chef* *de cuisine* for a head cook. *Capital, chapter,* and *decapitate* come more directly from *caput. Caption,* however, is from a different Latin word, *capere,* to seize or take. *Caption* was used in law for an arrest and then for part of a legal document like an indictment and then for a heading on a legal document and then for any kind of heading or subtitle, even one beneath a picture.

corporal. As the name for a military officer, *corporal* is derived from *caput,* head, but another *corporal,* as in "corporal punishment," comes from Latin *corpus,* body, which is also the source of *corpse,* a dead body; of *corporation,* a body of people; and of *corpulence,* too much body.

cad. To call someone a cad, like calling him a bounder, sounds old-fashioned these days. It means that he is ungentlemanly, behaves dishonorably toward women. The word goes back to Latin *caput,* head. The Latin word developed a diminutive *capitellum,* little head, which moved into French as *capdet,* little chief. The word moved into English as *cadet,* retaining military associations and designating particularly a trainee for the armed forces. In English colleges a hanger-on around the athletics fields was called a *cadet,* soon abbreviated to *cad*; and schoolboy snobbery associated the word with someone not a gentleman. In Scotland *cadet* became *caddie* or *caddy* to refer to an errand boy and then more specifically to a person who carries golf clubs.

precipice. *Caput*, head, is the source of another word less obviously related. Combined with the prefix *prae-*, before, *caput* produced French *precipice*, meaning a headlong fall; from the French, English acquired the word but gave it a new meaning, a steep, almost vertical, cliff or crag, a place where one might fall headlong.

caprice. By an interesting compounding in another language, *caprice* also goes back to *caput*. It comes from Italian *capriccio*, a shivering or a whim. The Italian word is a combination of Latin *caput*, head, and *riccio*, curl, and originally referred to a head with bristling hair. It became associated in meaning with Italian *capriolare*, from Latin *caper*, goat, meaning to leap. And modern *caprice* came to refer to a leap or turn of mind or emotion. In a different application, Italian *capriolare* produced *cabriolet*, for a light two-wheeled carriage that perhaps could leap along.

cadence. Latin *cadere*, to fall, is behind a number of English words. *Cadence* refers to the fall of the voice in speaking, but more generally to any inflection or modulation in tone or the measured beat in dancing or marching. The Italian form, *cadenza*, refers to a brilliant solo passage in music. Latin combined the prefix *de-* with *cadere* to produce *decidere,* to fall down or away, and this was the source of English *decay* and *decadence* and *deciduous.* A deciduous tree is one whose leaves fall off annually.

curriculum. Latin *currere* meant to run, and *curriculum* was a race. A curriculum, a course of study or a collection of them, may sometimes seem like a race. *Current, cursory, concur,* and *course* all echo their origin in the verb for running.

eloquent. Latin *loqui,* to speak, is the root for a variety of English words. A loquacious person is likely to talk too much. *Loqui* combined with *con-,* together, produced *colloquial,* conversational or informal when applied to language. *Solus,* alone, and *loqui* are behind *soliloquy,* a solo speech, and *circum-,* around, and *loqui* are behind *circumlocution.* A ventriloquist speaks from the belly (*loqui* plus *venter,* belly). *Loqui* combined in Latin with *e-,* out, to produce *eloqui,* to speak out, the root for *eloquent* and *elocution.*

fetish. Latin *facere,* to make, in various forms—*fec, fac, fact, fect, fy*—is behind many English words. English adopted one form as the word *fact.* Combined with *manus,* hand, *facere* produced *manufacture*; with *petra,* stone, *petrify*; with *fortis,* strong, *fortify*; with *magnus,* large, *magnify.* Other words deriving from *facere* are *facile, efficient, facsimile, effect. Facere* led to Latin *facti-*

cius, artificial, from which developed Portuguese *feitico* and French *faetiche,* for a charm or device for sorcery. These led to English *fetish,* which has generalized to refer to anything held as an object of unreasoning devotion—making a *fetish* of clothes or cleanliness or long fingernails. In psychiatry it refers to a nonsexual object—a glove or shoe—that excites erotic feelings.

segue. Latin *sequi,* to follow, is behind *sequel, sequence, consequence, obsequies.* With *per-,* through, it produced *persecute,* to follow through and harass or annoy a victim. With *ex-,* out, it produced *execute,* to follow out or carry out, and *executive.* Italian *seguire,* to follow, came from it and led to a musical term, *segue,* a direction to proceed to the next movement without a break. The term was adopted in English and has recently been generalized, especially by radio announcers, to refer to any uninterrupted movement: "The guitar player segued to the final chorus."

venue. Latin *venire,* to come, appears in English words especially in the forms *ven* and *vent. Convention, venire* plus *con-,* together, refers to people coming together. *Venire* with *circum-,* around, produces *circumvent*; with *pre-,* before, *prevent*; with *inter-,* between, *intervene. Venue* came into the language in the nineteenth century as a law term, to designate the locality in which a case must be tried.

Lawyers might seek a change of venue. The term has generalized to refer to any location of an event, and seems currently to be overused to refer to the site of a rock concert or a boxing match.

punctuate. Latin *pungere* meant to pierce, and *punctus* was a point. English *point* derives from *punctus* through Old French. A *puncture* is a perforation made with a sharp point. A *pungent* taste may have a sharp, stinging quality, and a *pungent* remark may seem pointed. The marks used to separate elements in writing are sometimes called points, and *punctuation* is the process of using them. *Punctilious* indicates careful, perhaps overcareful, observance of points of conduct or manners. *Punctual* describes observance of a specified point in time.

aggravate. *Aggravate* comes from Latin *ad-*, to, plus *gravis*, heavy. *Grave* doubts are weighty; a *grave* burden is heavy. In space travel the lack of *gravity* is called weightlessness. Preoccupation with the history of *aggravate*, however, has caused problems about its usage. A tradition going back to the late nineteenth century holds that the word should be used only to mean make worse, not to mean provoke, irritate, or anger. The objection is based partly on an attempt to preserve the Latin meaning behind the word. Grant White's 1870 usage book says that the word "means merely to add weight to." But the less literal meanings, to annoy or irritate, are currently standard.

unique. *Unique* is another example of a word whose origin keeps raising questions about its usage. The origin of the word is fairly obvious, from Latin *unus,* meaning one, and *unique* once meant "only," as in "his unique son." Some users of the language feel that this earlier meaning and the word's origin make the word a so-called absolute—like *full, perfect, final, complete, waterproof.* The notion, with a certain amount of logic, is that a glass can't be fuller than full or a coat more waterproof than waterproof. Certainly we think of some such words as incomparable. If we say "very dead" or "very pregnant," we're trying to be funny. By the same reasoning something that is unique is the only one and can't be more or less unique. But the meaning of *unique* has clearly changed. Today the word may mean something like in a class by itself or unparalleled, but most often it just means remarkable or is an almost meaningless term of general praise.

contact. Like *aggravate* and *unique, contact* is interesting because its ancestry is frequently cited as a reason for restricting its usage. It comes from Latin *tangere,* to touch, which is the root of English *tangible* and *tangent. Tangere,* with the prefix *com-,* together, produced English *contact*, a noun. In the 1920s, however, the noun developed use as a verb meaning get in touch with or communicate with. It had wide use, especially in business, but the use also was widely criticized, partly by citing the word's origin and insisting that the verb involves physical touching. According to the argument, you can't contact somebody by telephone or by writing a letter. Invoking a permanent attachment of a word to its origin, of course, ignores patterns of semantic change, and *contact* has become a standard English verb in spite of objections and its overuse.

onion. Latin *unio*, union, is the ancestor of both *onion*, the name of a plant, and *union*, a name for a large pearl. And *unio*, like *unique* or *unit*, goes back to Latin *unus*, one. *Onion* has developed some kind of association with sanity or wisdom to produce phrases like "off one's onion" or "know one's onions." *Unio*, reflecting its source in *unus*, came to refer to a single onion or a single pearl, which perhaps looked like a small onion. In *Hamlet*, King Claudius throws a union into his cup,

> Richer than that which four successive kings
> In Denmark's crown have worn.

accost. Latin *costa*, rib or side, was the origin of Old French *coste*, and then English *coast*, the side or edge of the shore. *Costa*, with the prefix *ad-*, to, is also behind *accost*, which formerly meant to be alongside of and then came to mean to approach or greet. The word also specialized to mean to solicit for sexual purposes. Shakespeare plays with *accost* in *Twelfth Night;* Sir Toby explains to Sir Andrew, "'accost' is front her, board her, woo her, assail her."

ambulance. Latin *ambulare*, to walk, is the origin of French *hôpitals ambulants*, literally walking hospitals. English adopted the name without the *hôpitals*. *Amble*, to move or walk at a leisurely pace, is another derivative of *ambulare*. And another is *perambulator*, *pram* in England, which requires walking from a pusher but no walking for a child.

corset. Latin *corpus*, body, became *cors* in Old French, which produced a diminutive, *corselet*, for armor for the body and then English *corset* for a close-fitting undergarment. A different diminutive is behind *corpuscle*, and another variant produced *corpulent*. *Corsage* also came through the French to refer to the bodice of a woman's dress and then to flowers that might be worn there.

custom. *Custom* is derived from Latin *consuescere*, to become accustomed. A custom is a usual practice or usage, a habit. It developed a specialized meaning, however, to refer to rent or services paid to a feudal lord and then, in the plural, to duties imposed by a government on imported goods. *Customer,* from the same root, refers to a person who buys in a store, especially one who buys regularly or customarily. The word has generalized in an interesting way to refer to any person one has to deal with, as in "he's a rough customer." *Custom* has also developed an interesting contemporary use, probably as a shortening of *custom-built,* built to the order or specifications of a customer; a *custom house* is presumably a custom-built house. As an advertiser's adjective, however, *custom* has become almost meaningless. Used to describe mass-produced automobiles or furniture or lingerie, *custom* expresses only vague approval and joins other favorites of admen, like *improved, better, extra,* or *special.*

gaudy. The Spanish architect Antonio Gaudí i Cornet, who died in 1926, is frequently credited with giving his name to the word *gaudy,* presumably because his designs were gaudy. Actually the word was around long before 1926, deriving from Latin *gaudere,* to rejoice. A famous medieval student song begins "Gaudeamus igitur," "Let us therefore rejoice." *Gaudere* also produced Middle English *gaude,* a jewel or ornament. *Gaudy* has retained the root meaning from rejoicing but has also specified the sense of *gaud* to suggest exaggerated ornament or tasteless decoration. Shakespeare uses the word in the root sense when Antony proposes to Cleopatra, "Come, let's have one other gaudy night." In English colleges an annual celebratory dinner held for old members is called a gaudy. Dorothy Sayers's mystery novel that takes place in an English college is titled *Gaudy Night*.

inoculate. English *oculist* and *binoculars* come from Latin *oculus,* eye. Latin *inoculare* was a combination of the prefix *in-,* into, and *oculus,* which also meant bud, and it was adopted in English as a gardening term, *inoculate,* for inserting an eye or bud of one plant into another for propagation. It acquired a new use at the time of the first inoculation against smallpox, for the inserting of the seed of a germ or virus into the body to produce immunity.

literal. Latin *litera,* letter, produced English *letter, literature,* and *literal,* to refer to something based on the exact words of an original—"a literal translation" or "a literal interpretation of the law." In its adverb form, however, the word has become an intensive with an almost opposite meaning—"She literally flew into the room" or "He was literally dead after the long hike." *Virtually* has shifted in a similar way.

mirror. The origin of its name suggests one of the major uses of a mirror. *Mirror* comes from Latin *mirari,* to wonder at. The Latin produced *admire,* which once meant to marvel or wonder at, and *miracle,* an object of wonder, as well as *mirror*, apparently because a mirror was used for self-admiration or wonder. Ambrose Bierce, in *The Devil's Dictionary*, defines admiration as "our polite recognition of another's resemblance to ourselves."

napkin. *Napkin* goes back to Latin *mappa*, which named a tablecloth but also named the cloth on which maps were printed. Two words in Old French derived from *mappa: mappemonde*, map of the world, and *nape*, tablecloth. From one of these we get modern *map* and from the other modern *napery*, household linen. Adding the diminutive ending *-kin* produced *napkin*, a smaller cloth used in a table setting, a serviette in England. But in England a *napkin* or *nappy* is a baby's diaper.

notorious. The Latin verb *noscere*, to know, produced a number of English words—*note, notable, notice, notify,* for example. It also is behind *notorious*, which for a long time meant well known or publicly discussed, with no unfavorable connotations. Perhaps from its association with unsavory nouns, however—in phrases like "notorious sinners"—*notorious* has come to mean widely and unfavorably known. Current dictionaries even list words like *infamous, disreputable*, or *scandalous* as synonyms.

pale. Latin *palus*, a stake or prop, was the source in English of both *pole* and *pale*, originally a stake driven into the ground or a picket in a fence. The word generalized to refer to any limit or boundary and then to an enclosed place or a district or region within determined bounds, as in "beyond the pale." The English Pale was the part of Ireland in which English law was acknowledged. The adjective *pale* is a quite different word, from Latin *pallere*, to be pale.

parlor. Latin *parlare*, to speak, is the root for *parley*, *parlance*, *parole*, *parliament*. It is also the base for *parlor*; originally a parlor was considered a place for conversation, for entertaining guests. In America *parlor* developed a number of uses in combinations: *parlor car*, *parlor stove*, *parlor organ*. Most of these words, like the objects they name, have gone out of common use. *Drawing room* is short for *withdrawing room*, originally a room where one withdraws after a meal.

pigeon. Latin *pipere* meant to peep or chirp and is the source of English *pipe*, a hollow straw or wood or metal pipe used for making alleged musical sounds, and the many extended meanings of *pipe*. A *pipe* is a boatswain's whistle, a tube and bowl used for smoking, a concrete or metal or wooden tube for conveying water or oil or other fluids, or in slang something easy to accomplish. It has verb uses, including *pipe up* and *pipe down*. Old French *pijon,* for a chirping bird, came from *pipere,* and English *pigeon* was derived from the French. *Pidgin,* as in *pidgin English,* is an entirely different word, a Chinese version of how English *business* is pronounced. Pidgin English developed as a simplified form of the language that could be used in trade or business.

poll. Latin *poll,* head, developed a number of meanings in English. It can mean head—"He wore a small cap on his gray poll"—or as a verb it can mean to cut off a head, especially of an animal, or to cut wool or hair or horns from a head. *Polled* can mean bald or dehorned. The notion of counting heads is behind the most common use of the word today, to refer to a canvass of voters for an election or to any counting of votes or opinions.

pugnacious. Latin *pugnus* meant fist, and from it the Latin verb *pugnare,* to fight, developed, and later the English word *pugnacious. Pugnare* also is behind Latin *pugil,* a boxer, and English *pugilism* and *pugilist,* abbreviated in slang to *pug,* for a boxer, especially a small-time one, and by extension for any young tough. A quite different *pug* is probably a variant of *puck,* a fairy or elf or sprite, and was a term of endearment and also meant something like a little imp in reference to a monkey or fox or little dog. The small dog called a pug looks like a bulldog, and a pug nose is turned up at the tip like that of a pug dog.

quest. Latin *quaerere,* to ask or seek, was adopted in English as *query* but was also the source for a number of words involving asking or searching: *quest, question, inquest, conquest, request, require, exquisite,* and many others. *Quest,* primarily a search, as medieval knights went on a quest for the Holy Grail, developed an interesting variation. Since hounds were involved in a hunt or quest for game, the word *quest* came to be used for the baying of hounds at the sight of game. In Sir Thomas Malory's *Le Morte d'Arthur* Sir Palomides is following a "questing beast that had in shape a head like a serpent's head, and a body like a leopard, buttocks like a lion, and footed like an hart; and in his body there was such a noise as it had been the noise of thirty couple hounds questing" (9.12).

radical. *Radish* and *radical* have the same origin. Both go back to Latin *radix,* meaning root. A radish is an edible root; a radical originally went to the root of a matter, to fundamentals. In politics, however, *radical* has shifted to a meaning almost opposite that of its origin. In the late eighteenth century activists sometimes called "root-and-branch men" advocated broad changes going back to the root of things. They were called radicals because of their concern for fundamentals, but they were remembered as extremists, and *radical* became associated with any extreme position. Today the term is mainly derogatory, having little denotational significance. We can have radical leftists or radical conservatives.

rustic. Latin *rus, ruris,* country, is the origin of *rural* and *rustic,* but *rustic* has developed uncomplimentary connotations beyond its basic meaning to refer to something rural. It can mean simple or plain or artless, but it can also refer to a person, suggesting awkwardness or even boorishness. To rusticate is to move or retire to the country, but sometimes *rusticate* suggests a kind of deterioration. And in England *rusticate* has developed a special meaning to refer to suspension from a college as a punishment.

tact. Latin *tactus,* from *tangere,* to touch, is the source of English *tactile* and *tangible,* capable of being perceived by touch, and *tangent,* touching. There is no evidence for the notion that *tango* is derived from *tangere* because the partners in the dance touch each other. *Tact* originally referred in English to the sense of touch, and the ability to say or do the appropriate thing is perhaps like a sense of touch.

torture. Latin *torquere,* twist, produced English *torque,* a twisting or rotating force. It is also behind Late Latin *tortura,* twisting or writhing or torment. The rack was a popular early form of torture, and involved wrenching and twisting the body. With a different emphasis *tortuous* developed for a circuitous route or a devious argument. The root meaning, twist, combined with various prefixes to produce other English words: *extort*, to twist out, especially to get money through threats or violence; *distort*, to twist away or out of shape; *contort*, to twist with or on itself; and *retort*, a remark turned back on someone. *Torch* also developed from *torquere* because torches often consisted of faggots or reeds twisted together.

tradition. Latin *traditio* was a surrender or a delivery, and *tradition* in English was originally a surrender or betrayal. It was also one kind of delivery, a handing down of information or custom from generation to generation, which is the common current meaning. *Traitor* and *treason* have the same root, echoing the meaning of *traditio* as a surrender or betrayal.

vault. Latin *volvere*, to turn around or roll, is the source of many English words. *Volume* was originally a roll of parchment, a scroll. *Revolve, evolve, convolution,* and *involve* all reflect the sense of turning or winding. *Volvere* also produced Old French *vaulte*, an arched roof, and from it English *vault*, with a variety of uses. The English word named an arched roof but also any arched room or chamber, especially underground, and hence a secure room in a bank or a burial chamber for the dead. The verb *vault,* meaning to jump or leap over, is closer to the word's Latin origin.

virtual. Latin *vir,* man, is the source of many English words, mainly flattering to the notion of manhood, *virile, virtue, virtuoso. Virtual* started out that way, pertaining to a real or potential force, as when Milton wrote, "Fomented by his virtual power," that is, power filled with virtue. But the meaning has shifted so that today *virtual* usually means almost the opposite of *real* or *actual,* suggesting that something is similar to or almost as good as something else. Advertisers have found *virtually* an especially useful word, to give what is really a false impression: "This soap leaves laundry virtually spotless" or "This washing machine is virtually trouble free." Compare the development of the meaning of *literally. Virtual reality* is a recent term to designate a computer-generated simulation of an environment, and in the cybersphere *virtual* is employed to describe temporary extension by computer software, as in a *virtual disk* or *virtual memory on a hard disk.*

vivid. Latin *vivere,* to live, and *vita,* life, are the roots of a variety of English words. *Vivid* colors are lively and clear. A *vivacious* person is also lively, full of *vitality.* A *revival* is a restoration of life, to an unconscious person or an old play. *Survive* comes from Latin *super-*, above, and *vivere*. *Vivisection* combines Latin *vivus*, alive, and *secare*, to cut, to describe surgery on a living animal. *Viviparous*, the bearing of living young, comes from Latin *vivus* and *parere*, to produce.

CHAPTER 2

Adapting Latin

ENGLISH USED LATIN IN A VARIETY OF WAYS to expand its stock of words. Often, as the previous chapter illustrates, it took a basic Latin word and developed a variety of English words from it. Sometimes it simply adopted a word, changing its meaning only slightly. *Appendix*, *climax*, *epitome*, *delirium*, and *axis* came into the language in their Latin forms with little change in meaning. Latin *datum*, plural *data*, is a form of the verb *dare*, to give, and meant a gift or what is given. English adopted it with no change in form but shifted meaning to refer specifically to facts or information from which conclusions can be drawn. Latin *dactylus,* finger and also the fruit of the date palm, was the source of English *date.* But it was also adopted as *dactyl,* the name of a poetic foot, presumably because of the three joints in a finger. It also combined with Greek *ptero,* feather or flying, to produce *pterodactyl.* One of the most common ways of adapting Latin to usual English word forms was dropping or changing a Latin ending. Latin *conjectural-is* became English *conjectural;* Latin *exotic-us* became English *exotic.* Or Latin *conspicu-us* became English *conspicuous,* and Latin *extern-us* became English *extern-al.* English speakers showed imagination and ingenuity in adapting Latin to expand their language.

alligator. The Latin name for a lizard, *lacerta,* became *el legarto* in Spanish, which was easily adapted by Americans to produce a name for its giant lizards. For unclear reasons, the name for the animal was applied in America to the avocado, which became an *alligator pear,* perhaps because of the rough skin of the fruit. *Avocado* comes from a native Mexican word, *ahuactl,* which originally meant testicle but was applied to the fruit and became Spanish *avogado.*

ampersand. The sign for *and,* &, is a representation of Latin *et,* or perhaps the first letter of *et.* The name

comes from an old way of explaining the character, "&
per se (that is, by itself) and." Children were taught to re-
cite the alphabet as "A *per se* A" for "A by itself A," "B *per
se* B," and so on. When they came to the end of the alphabet and the character &, they said "& *per se* and," which
became *ampersand*.

coward. Latin *cauda*, tail, produced Old French
couard and then English *coward*, for someone who turns
tail, perhaps with tail between legs.

fanatic. Latin *fanum* named a temple, and Latin *fanati-
cus*, of the temple, also meant something like inspired by
divinity. In English *fanatic* suggests more than inspiration, excessive zeal, or enthusiasm. It is usually a pejora-
tive term. Abbreviated to *fan* it is more neutral, designating a supporter not necessarily fanatic—a baseball fan or
a member of a singer's fan club. Latin also combined
fanum with the prefix *pro-*, before, to make *profanus*, outside the temple, hence not sacred, the source of English
profane.

fanfare. In Latin *fanfaron* was a name for a braggart or
blusterer, and a *fanfare* can perhaps be thought of as a
bluster of trumpets, a showy display.

focus. Latin *focus* named a fireplace or hearth. In 1604
the German astronomer Johannes Kepler adopted the word
for scientific uses, particularly to specify a point at which

rays of light or heat come together. The word has generalized beyond its various uses in mathematics and physics to refer to any center of interest or attraction, perhaps reflecting the sense of a fireplace as the center of a household. Through its Old French form *fouaille*, *focus* also produced English *fuel*.

frugal. Latin *frux*, fruit, is behind English *fruit* with all its meanings; but also in some of its forms it is the source of *frugal*. Latin *frugalis* meant fit for fruit or food and hence proper or worthy, and English *frugal* came to mean economical or inexpensive.

gout. The painful disease, a form of arthritis especially affecting the smaller bones of the foot, has been popularly associated with high living and nineteenth-century gentlemen fond of a second bottle of claret. The name, however, reflects an earlier, no-more-accurate theory of the causes for the disease. *Gout* comes through French from Latin *gutta*, a drop. According to the medieval theory, the bodily humors could flow about, and morbid material might escape and drop to the joints of the foot. The *gutta* or drop caused discomfort. The French word *goût*, taste, is spelled the same way but is not related to the disease.

hearse. Latin *hirpex* and later Old French *herce* were names for a harrow, used in cultivating soil. The ancient harrow was triangular, and the triangular frame used to hold funeral candles looked like it and took its name as *herse*. Then the word was used for the frame carrying a coffin; and when carriages were introduced for funerals, *hearse* was applied to them. *Rehearse* has the same origin, with *re-*, again, plus *herce*, with the suggestion that practice involves harrowing a play or a speech again.

hoosegow. Latin *judicare*, to judge, is the root of Spanish *juzgar*, to judge, and *juzgado*, sentenced. The Mexican pronunciation of *juzgado* sounded like *hoosegow*. In the American West the word came to be applied to the place where someone went when he was sentenced, or *juzgado*.

humble. Eating humble pie implies some acknowledgment of error, some humbleness, but the origin of the word has nothing to do with humility or humbleness. The Latin word *lumbus*, meaning loin, is behind the Middle English word *umbles* or sometimes *numbles*, the entrails of a deer. Pie made from umbles was provided for servants after a hunt. Humble pie was made from the least palatable parts of the deer, and eating it was self-effacing, like eating crow, also not considered ideal fare. *Humble*, meaning modest or unpretentious, is a quite different word. It comes from Latin *humus*, which meant earth, as it still does, and *humilis*, meaning on the ground and also small or low. The same roots produced *humility* and *exhume*.

hybrid. The Latin name for the offspring of a tame sow and a wild boar was *hybrida*. English adopted the word and generalized it to refer to anything of mixed origin. More recently a combination of folk etymology and advertising ingenuity has touted hybrid corn as *Hi-bred* corn.

innuendo. A nod can have the same effect as an indirect remark, an insinuation, often derogatory. Latin *innuere* meant to nod. Besides referring generally to an indirect reference, *innuendo* has a specific use in law to refer to explanatory material introduced in a suit, especially in a case of libel or slander.

mob. Mob is an abbreviation of Latin *mobile vulgus*, a moveable crowd. It was shortened to *mobile* in the sixteenth century and to *mob* in the seventeenth, but *mob* was considered slang and was slow to gain recognition as standard English. Jonathan Swift in 1712 lamented: "I have done my utmost for some years past to stop the progress of *mobb* and *banter*, but have been plainly borne down by numbers." Swift was not successful. The *mob* today may refer simply to the people, the masses. In military slang early in the twentieth century it referred to a military unit, a regiment, a battalion. In Australia a mob can be a gang of toughs or a band of sheep. Most often today *mob* is used for the rabble, a disorderly group, and especially in the United States it is likely to designate an organized criminal group like the Mafia.

omelet. Latin *lamella,* a small or thin plate, became *l'allemelle* in French, and perhaps by confusion with *allemette,* the thin blade of a sword, came to be spelled *omelette,* also *omelet.* Presumably because of the thin, flat shape of the beaten-egg dish, the word for a thin blade or plate was applied to the dish and then to the eggs cooked in it. More directly *lamella* was the source for English *laminate,* to cover with a thin layer.

pagan. *Pagan* is a term, usually contemptuous, applied to someone who is not Christian or Jewish or Moslem by somebody who is. It developed, however, from words not associated with religion. Latin *pagus,* country, produced *paganus,* a peasant or villager, as distinct from *miles,* a soldier. Early Christians adopted the term to refer to any non-Christian, and the word generalized so that it now often means simply not religious.

palliate. A rectangular cloak draped over the left shoulder and around the body was called a *pallium* by the Romans. In the Roman Catholic Church a circular white wool band worn on the shoulder by archbishops is still called a *pallium.* Latin also developed the word *palliatus* to mean covered with a cloak, which produced English *palliate*, to ease pain or to make a crime or offense seem less serious than it is, in a sense to cloak it.

pastor. Latin *pascere*, to feed, produced English *pastor*, a shepherd who feeds his flock. The term easily transferred to name a clergyman or priest who is like a shepherd leading a congregation. *Pascere* is also the root of *pasture*, an area suitable for grazing or feeding animals.

pavilion. Cloth spread as a canopy or tent looked like a butterfly when the wind blew and got its name from the Latin name for a butterfly, *papillio*. The word was used in England especially to describe the tents occupied by knights for jousting or tournaments. The French name for a butterfly is *papillon*, which is behind English *papillote*, for anyone who needs a name for the little paper frill placed on the end of a lamb chop by some restaurants or likes fish cooked *en papillote*.

prestige. In the eighteenth century *prestige* referred to a conjuring trick, an illusion, a deception. This meaning, now obsolete, directly reflected the word's origin, in Latin *praestigium*, juggler's trick. Now the word has lost these earlier meanings and denotes esteem or reputation or influence, not necessarily acquired through deception. Latin is also behind *prestigiator*, a juggler or conjurer, which was used in the sixteenth century, but which was modified to *prestidigitator*, apparently by combining *preste*, nimble, with Latin *digitus*, finger.

prude. English *proud* comes from Latin *prodesse*, to be of value, through Old French *prud*. French also produced *prudefemme*, a worthy and excellent woman. English adopted *prude*, but its meaning rapidly degenerated to refer to a person, especially a woman, having or affecting an attitude of extreme propriety, especially in sexual matters.

puce. The Latin name for a flea is *pulex*, and presumably at least some fleas had the brownish purple color we now call puce. *Pulex* was modified to Old French *pulce*, a flea, and then to French *couleur puce*, flea colored, and *puce* was adopted in English. English *pulicose* is flea-infested or flea-bitten.

quality. *Quality* comes from Latin *qualis*, meaning what kind or what sort, and refers to a characteristic or element or attribute of something. Blueness or hardness or impracticality or stupidity might be qualities. There can be good qualities and bad qualities. As an adjective, however, *quality* has come to suggest only good qualities, as in *quality education* or *quality paperbacks* or *quality performance*.

quarantine. Latin *quadraginta*, meaning forty, also came to mean forty days, specifically referring to Lent. As *quarantine* it specified forty days that ships suspected of carrying disease were required to remain in isolation. The length of time for this isolation came to vary, according to the nature of the suspected disease, but the term remained and extended to refer to any enforced isolation, usually to prevent the spread of a disease.

restaurant. In the early nineteenth century, *restaurant* developed in English, emphasizing that the purpose of eating is to strengthen and restore. The word, with the same roots as *restore*, goes back to Latin *restaurare*, to make strong.

ruminate. *Ruminate*, to ponder or meditate, has come a long way through a cow's stomach to its current meaning. Latin *rumen*, throat or gullet, was adopted in the eighteenth century as the name for the first and largest stomach of a cow, deer, camel, or other cud-chewing animal. Animals that regurgitate grass or other food, chew it, and then swallow it again are ruminants, and what they chew is a cud, from Anglo-Saxon *cwudu*, a ball. A cow's procedure, "chewing it over," has been generalized to mean thinking it over, pondering, reflection.

scintillate. Latin *scintilla* is the word for a spark, and a scintillating wit is one that flashes or sparkles. In English *scintilla* has generalized to refer to a trace or particle or tiny amount. *Scintillate* is seldom used in English except to refer to an intellect, or occasionally a star. The Latin word became *étincelle* in French, which was picked up in English without the first letter and became *tinsel*, which sparkles on Christmas trees.

screw. The word *screw* is interesting because it shifted from its somewhat unsavory origins to respectability and then picked up dubious modern slang meanings. The word comes from Latin *scrofa*, sow, influenced by *scrobis*, vulva, which led to Old French *escroue*, a hole in which a screw turns. The original meaning survives in English in *female screw*, a socket or grooved cylinder in which a male screw fits. But the term came to be used primarily for any kind of nail with spiral grooves used for fastening things together. And then by metaphorical association dozens of other meanings developed. The propellor on a boat worked like a screw and came to be called a screw. A bit of tobacco in twisted paper became a screw. British slang made a key a screw, perhaps because it turned, and then a prison guard or turnkey became a screw. By the early eighteenth century the word had also regained its earlier improper meanings and had become a more-or-less taboo word for sexual intercourse. And this use influenced meanings like to cheat or force as in "put the screws on." Especially in England the notion of screwing someone out of money apparently led to the notion of *screw* meaning salary or pay and the notion of a *screw* as a miser—a meaning Dickens may have had in mind when he named Scrooge. Someone with a screw loose may be a screwball or just screwy. The uses relating to sex are currently less clearly improper than they were a generation ago.

scruple. In early Rome a *scrupulus* was a small pebble and also the smallest unit of weight. English adopted the word as *scruple,* as a term used by apothecaries for a small weight, twenty grains; that use is now obsolete. But the Latin word had also developed a figurative meaning, from the notion of an irritating sharp stone, as in a shoe, causing anxiety or doubt. Hamlet wonders if he is affected by "some craven scruple of thinking too precisely on the event."

soldier. These days soldiers are not often distinguished by their salaries, but the history of *soldier* suggests that through the ages soldiers were often mercenaries, associated with the pay they received. The word *soldier* goes back to Latin *solidus,* a piece of money.

spoil. In Latin *spolium* was hide stripped from an animal and then arms taken from a defeated foe. From this meaning the Latin verb *spoliare,* to plunder, developed. English *spoil* or *spoils* referred to anything taken by conquest from an enemy and then to profit or gain from a political victory, particularly the ability to make appointments. As a verb *spoil* developed more general meanings, to injure or damage, or to become rotten or tainted—what too many cooks do to the broth.

spouse. Latin *spondere* meant to make an agreement, and *sponsus* named a person who had promised something, a contractor. In English a *sponsor* of an event is a person who promises support. *Sponsus* and its feminine form *sponsa* also acquired more specific meanings for a man or woman who had been promised in marriage. These entered English as *spouse* and came to refer to either member of a married couple.

trivial. The Latin word *trivium* from *tri*, three, plus *via*, way, named a crossing of three roads. Later, in the Middle Ages, in deference to the sense of three in the word, it was applied to the first division of the liberal arts in the education system—grammar, rhetoric, and logic. The quadrivium followed—arithmetic, geometry, astronomy, and music. *Trivial* developed from the notion that the trivium was the more elementary program; the word meant commonplace or ordinary and then came to mean trifling or insignificant.

ubiquitous. Latin *ubi* means where, and *ubique* means everywhere. English *ubiquitous* keeps the Latin meaning. Another English word with the same meaning is also just a translation of its Latin roots. Latin *omnis*, all, plus *prae,* before, plus *esse,* to be, are the source for *omnipresent.*

vanilla. Latin *vagina,* sheath or case, was the origin of Spanish *vainilla,* a small pod, which became English *vanilla,* for the podlike vanilla bean. English also adopted Latin *vagina* with no change in spelling to name a sheathlike structure in anatomy or botany, especially in female mammals the canal leading from the vulva to the uterus.

vernacular. Latin *verna* was the name for a slave born in the household, and *vernaculus* developed to mean domestic or native. The vernacular is the native language of a country or place.

vice. Separate Latin roots are behind two English words, both spelled *vice.* Latin *vicis,* a change or alteration, produced *vice* to mean in the place of as part of a number of English compounds, *vice president* or *viceroy,* using the French *roi,* king. *Vicarious,* taking the place of another person or thing, has the same ancestry. *Vicar,* from the same Latin root, originally referred to a person delegated to perform as a substitute or deputy, and then became a title for various church offices. Latin *vitium,* a weakness or fault, however, is responsible for a different *vice.* Originally this *vice* signified a relatively innocent mistake or error. Chaucer used it to refer to a spelling mistake. But it also became the name for a popular character in Old English mystery plays, a representative of more serious weaknesses like fraud or envy or wrath. By Shakespeare's time *vice* could refer to any immorality or depravity; currently it has tended to refer particularly to prostitution, the concern of the vice squad. *Vicious* developed from Latin *vitiosus*, corrupt, full of faults. A vicious circle is a situation in which solving one problem produces another problem, and solving this leads back to the original problem, perhaps with new complications.

CHAPTER 3

The Greeks Had a Word

ALTHOUGH NEARLY HALF THE WORDS IN A large English dictionary derive from Latin, Greek also has been a significant influence on the language. With the introduction of Christianity, a number of words came into Old English from Greek: *apostle*, *pope*, and *psalter*. Many English words came from Greek through Latin and French. *Antipathy, atmosphere, crisis, anachronism, climax, cycle, enthusiasm, metaphor, parasite, phenomenon,* and *theory* came to English through Latin. But with the renewed study of Greek the Renaissance brought many new words into English directly from Greek: *acme, agnostic, anonymous, catastrophe, criterion, ephemeral, tonic.* To cope with the remarkable growth of science in modern times, the language has relied heavily on Greek for new terms. *Telephone, acronym, chlorine, pathos, anthropology, lexicographer,* and *panacea* all have Greek origins. The words in this chapter are other examples.

adamant. Greek combined *daman,* tame, with a prefix *a-,* not, to produce *adamant,* originally meaning something like "invincible." This was specialized to refer to the hardest iron or other metal, and English adopted it through French with this meaning. It is now usually general, especially poetic, to refer to unbreakable hardness.

agony. Intense mental or physical suffering or agony may have various causes, but the origin of *agony* suggests that the stress of competition may be one source. Greek *agon,* a contest for a prize, was adopted in English as a word for the conflict of characters in a drama. It also was modified to produce *agony,* suggesting that the struggles of a contest may cause pain. With a different emphasis *agon* acquired the prefix *anti,* against, to make *antagonize,* to contend against.

amethyst. The Greeks had a notion that a bluish or purple gem was a charm to prevent drunkenness. They therefore named the stone by combining *a-*, not, with *methuein*, to be intoxicated. Latin adopted the combination as *amethystus*.

blame. Greek *blasphemein*, to speak evil of, moved through Latin and French to become English *blaspheme*, to speak profanely or irreverently of sacred things. Through another French derivative, *blasmer*, it became English *blame*, to accuse or find fault or criticize.

cosmetics. Greek *kosmos* meant order or harmony, and is the source of English *cosmos*, the universe as an orderly and harmonious system, and also of compounds like *cosmography*, a description of the world. Developing in another direction *kosmos* produced Greek *kosmein*, to arrange or adorn, and then English *cosmetics*, which involves more adorning than arranging. *Cosmetics* has generalized beyond its references to improvements in physical beauty to refer to anything done superficially to make something seem better than it is.

cynic. In ancient Greece, Antisthenes, a pupil of Socrates, founded a sect of philosophers who considered virtue to be the only good and stressed independence from worldly needs and pleasures. The philosophy of the school changed, however, as its members became more critical of the rest of society and drifted into self-righteousness. The public found their attitudes offensive and gave them the nickname *cynics,* from the Greek word *kynikos,* meaning like a dog. Modern writers have frequently provided cynical definitions of *cynic.* Ambrose Bierce, in *The Devil's Dictionary,* defines a cynic as "a blackguard whose faulty vision sees things as they are, not as they ought to be." Oscar Wilde defines a cynic as "a man who knows the price of everything and the value of nothing."

dynamite. Current slang uses of *dynamite,* as a name for heroin or as a general term of approval—"it was a dynamite speech"—echo the word's origin in Greek *dynamis,* power.

epiphany. The word *epiphany* comes from Greek *epi,* upon, plus *phainein,* to show. *Epiphainein,* appearance or manifestation, became *epiphany,* a sudden appearance, especially of a god, and then a name for a festival honoring the appearance of a deity. The name was adopted for the Christian festival on January 6, also called Twelfth Day, indicating the manifestation of Christ, especially to the Magi. A more fanciful explanation of the origin of the word derives it from a legend about a fairy called Epiphania. She was supposed to watch over the three wise men on their trip following the star. But she got busy with household chores and forgot. As penance she walks through nurseries on Twelfth Night, providing toys for children.

female. In a male-oriented society the assumption is sometimes made that *female* was created to be a companion word for *male*, as if *fe-* were a prefix like *she* in *she-bear*. The word actually goes back to Greek *thelazein*, to suckle, and then with some sound changes Latin *felare*, to suck, and Latin *femina*, woman. Associations with *male* may have influenced the English form of the word.

glamor. *Glamor, glamour* in England, had no Hollywood glitter in its origins. It goes back ultimately to Greek *gramma*, something written, which produced Middle English *grammare* and *gramary*, which designated a study of language but extended to refer to all learning. Partly because of superstitious beliefs about the power of words, *gramary* also became a name for a magic spell or enchantment, and an alternate spelling, *glamour*, appeared. It meant magic or enchantment; Tennyson wrote:

> That maiden in the tale,
> Whom Gwydion made by glamour out of flowers.

A hint of mystery and enchantment still colors the meaning of modern *glamor*.

glossary. Indo-European **glogh*, a thorn, led to Greek *glochis*, a point, and then to Greek *glossa*, tongue, which came to refer to language and then to a word and explanation of a word. A glossary is a collection of glosses, a list of difficult or technical or foreign terms with explanations. Science also went back to the Greek word for tongue and named the space between the vocal chords in the larynx *glottis*. A less common scientific term derives from *glochis*, a point, and anything pointed is *glochidate*. A different *gloss* comes from Old Norse *glossi*, a blaze, and refers to a shiny or polished surface and by extension to minimizing or de-emphasizing an error, glossing it over.

gymnasium. Etymologically a gymnasium is a place for naked people. The word comes from Greek *gymnos*, naked, which produced *gymnazein*, to train naked. Ancient Greek athletes often competed in the nude. In the fifteenth century humanists extended the use of *gymnasium* beyond its application to a place for physical education, and it became the European name for a secondary school for students preparing to enter a university.

helicopter. A helicopter gets its name quite logically through French *hélicoptère* from Greek *helikos*, a spiral, plus *pleron*, wing. The ancestry of *autogiro* is equally plausible, from Greek *autos*, self, plus *gyros*, a circle.

heliotrope. The small purple flowers on the heliotrope plant turn to follow the sunlight. They apparently had the same habits in ancient Greece, and the Greeks combined *helios*, sun, and *trepien*, to turn, to produce *heliotropion* as the name for the flower. By extension *heliotrope* is sometimes used as another name for a heliograph, a device for signaling by flashing the sun's rays from a mirror. *Heliograph* derives from a combination of *helios* with Greek *graphein*, to write.

hyperbole. Greek *ballein*, throw, combined with the prefix *hyper*, over, to produce *hyperbole*, literally to overthrow. Or, as it came to be used, *hyperbole* is exaggeration, usually for effect, not meant to be taken literally.

hysteria. The ancient Greeks thought that women more than men were subject to uncontrolled emotional outbursts and assumed that hysteria was caused by disturbances of the uterus. The Greek word for the uterus was *hystera*. The word with its original meaning is preserved in *hysterectomy*, surgical removal of the uterus.

icon. Greek *eikon*, image or figure, was adopted in English as *icon* with its original meaning but also with specific application in the church to a sacred image or picture of Jesus or Mary or a saint. In its more general sense it produced *iconoclast*, for a person who attacks traditional ideas or institutions. In the computer age, however, *icon* has specialized again and come to refer to a small image on a screen representing a disk drive, a command, a file, or a software program.

intoxicate. The Greek word *toxon* was the name for a bow, and the poison with which Greek archers tipped their arrows was called *toxicon*, which was generalized in Latin to produce *toxicum*, for any kind of poison. The bartender who says "Name your poison" is probably being more literal than he realizes, echoing that *intoxication* developed to mean something like "full of poison." The state of intoxication has had linguistic fascination for users of English, and Wentworth and Flexner in *Dictionary of American Slang* observe that in English "the concept having the most slang synonyms is *drunk*." They list 335 examples—*plastered, smashed, tipsy, fuddled,* and so on—and also a considerable number of modifying expressions to specify the degree or variety of intoxication such as *falling-down, blind, crying, as a skunk.*

jot. *Iota,* the ninth letter in the Greek alphabet, was thought of as the smallest letter, and its name was adopted in English to mean a very small quantity. *Yodh* was the smallest letter in the Hebrew alphabet, and its name also is apparently behind *iota* and also English *jot,* meaning a small or trifling amount. English also developed another word for an insignificant amount from the word *title,* creating *tittle* as the name for a dot used as a diacritical mark, above the letters *i* and *j,* for example. And somehow the old word *wight,* a person or human being, was the source for *whit*, another word for the smallest particle. So in English something can be not worth an iota or a jot or a tittle or a whit, or all four.

kudos. English adopted Greek *kydos*, glory or fame, in the nineteenth century as university slang. It was regarded as a singular mass noun like *glory, acclaim, prestige,* or *renown* in expressions like "He gained a little kudos for his performance." The word became popular with journalists in the 1920s, and since its final *s* makes it look like a plural, it was treated as a plural—"He won many kudos for his performance." And then by back formation a singular *kudo* appeared, rejected by some usage guides, although *kudos* as a plural seems established.

melancholy. Greek *melas*, black, and *chole*, bile, were combined as *melancholia*, the name for black bile, one of the four humors accounting for the temperament of human beings. Elizabethans attributed depression to an excess of black bile, and melancholy was looked on as a serious disease. Robert Burton's long treatise *The Anatomy of Melancholy* is a medical work that expands to become a broad philosophical and literary comment.

mystery. *Mystery* goes back ultimately to Greek *myein*, to shut the eyes, which led to Latin *mysterium*, a secret or secret worship. A different English *mystery* came from Latin *ministerium*, office or occupation. Middle English *misterie* or *mysterie* was the name for a trade or craft, and the medieval plays produced in England by the trade guilds were mystery plays, but not plays about mysteries.

onomatopoeia. *Onomatopoeia* is a Greek word, literally name-making or self-made, to describe the creation of a word by imitating the sound of the object or action named—*buzz, fizz, tinkle*. Such words are also called echoic.

orchid. Neither its beauty nor its status as a symbol of luxury has anything to do with the name of the orchid, which depends on the shape of its roots. The double roots of the plant were thought to resemble testicles, and *orchid* comes from Greek *orchis,* the word for testicles.

oxymoron. Two Greek words, *oxys,* meaning sharp, and *moros,* meaning foolish or dull, are the source of *oxymoron,* the name for a figure of speech that combines two opposites like the meaning of its Greek roots: *cruel kindness, wise fool, thunderous silence, conspicuous by his absence.* The word and the figure have had a recent revival for satirical purposes, the combining of two ideas that are not necessarily opposites but are thought of as opposites when the combination is labeled an oxymoron. Calling *business ethics* an oxymoron reveals an attitude toward the way businesses are run. Or consider *military intelligence* or *family vacation.* Slightly different are oxymorons that are self-canceling if we consider their literal meaning, although they have become conventional phrases: *Pacific storm, jumbo shrimp, original copy, numb feeling, plastic glasses, green blackboards*. A related figure, which has not enjoyed a modern revival and remains fairly obscure in the archives of classical rhetoric, is *zeugma*, joining two words so that one is used accurately and the other ironically: *waging war and peace*.

parasite. Greek *parasitos*, one who eats beside or at the table of another, was a combination of *para*, beside, and *sitos*, food. In ancient Greece a *parasite* was a person who flattered a host in return for free meals. The modern English meaning is more general. A parasite can be any person who lives at the expense of another, or it can be a plant, like mistletoe, that is sustained by another organism.

pedagogue. Greek *pais*, child, plus *agein*, to lead, produced *paedagogus* in Latin, a slave who took children to school, and *pedagogue* in English for a teacher. The Greek root also led to French *pedant*, a schoolmaster, and English adopted it. In English both *pedagogue* and *pedant* have acquired some unfavorable connotations, suggesting a dogmatic teacher, one who stresses trivial points of learning and may stress adherence to arbitrary rules. Combining *agein*, to lead, with *demos*, people, produced *demagogue*, which has also acquired unfavorable connotations, as a would-be leader of the people appealing to emotions and prejudice in order to achieve selfish ends.

pumpkin. Greek *pepon* meant cooked by the sun or ripe. Through French it produced early English *pumpion*, which became *pumpkin* for the round fruit, which is not eaten until it is ripe. "He is some pumpkins" in slang is a compliment.

rhinoceros. The Greeks created the name for the rhinoceros by combining *rhis*, nose, and *keros*, bone, to make *rhinokeros*. Obviously the Greeks were impressed by the large horn on the animal's snout, which in more recent times has led to the near extinction of some species. Superstitious belief in the aphrodisiac powers of powder ground from the horn has stimulated widespread poaching.

sarcophagus. The ancient Greeks created their word for a coffin from *sarkos*, flesh, and *phagein*, to eat. Their *sarkophagos* was made of a kind of limestone that was thought to cause rapid disintegration of the coffin's contents.

school. Modern students probably feel that the meaning of *school* has changed significantly from its origin in Greek *schole*, meaning leisure. The word perhaps reflects leisurely discussions of philosophers like Plato. It moved into Latin as *schola,* meaning school. In "a school of minnows," the school is an entirely different word, from Dutch *school,* meaning a crowd. A related Old English word *scolu,* a band of people, produced another name for a group of fish, *shoal.*

stoic. The Greek philosopher Zeno taught under a colonnade in Athens, in the Stoa Poecile, the painted porch, near the Agora. *Stoa* or *stoikos* was the Greek word for a porch or colonnade, and the followers of Zeno were called Stoics from the porch where they gathered to hear Zeno. As a common noun, *stoic* has come to refer to a person following the austere doctrines of the philosophy, repressing emotions, showing patience in the face of adversity.

treasure. The Greek word for a store of valuables was *thesauros,* which through Old French gave English the word *treasure.* English, however, adopted the Greek word directly to name a collection of words, especially a book of synonyms, a *thesaurus.*

CHAPTER 4

Borrowing
Around the World

ALTHOUGH LATIN AND GREEK ARE BEHIND
thousands of English words, the language has
always been hospitable, and words in the current vocabulary have parents from all over the world.
Some we simply adopted: *sauna* from Finland, *kimono*
from Japan, *taboo* from Polynesia, *vodka* and *steppe* from
Russia, *khaki* and *shawl* from Persia, *banana* and *cork* from
Spain. Others we modified to fit our needs. For example,
an Australian aborigine word *bumarin* was adopted in
English as *boomerang* and began developing metaphorical

uses to refer to any scheme or project that recoils on its originator. Persian *Shah mat,* an exclamation used to celebrate victory in a chess game, came to the West with the game and was modified to *checkmate. Check* was associated with the game and the board on which it was played, a checkerboard, and then anything with a pattern of alternate squares, like a red-and-white-checked tablecloth. *Check* in chess meant power and control, and we can check a person's authority, which can mean either stop it or determine whether it exists. The person who controls money is an *exchequer* in England, and a check is an order to a bank to pay money. Following are some words borrowed from all over the world.

algebra. *Geometry* has a logical ancestry, coming from Greek *ge,* earth or land, and *metria,* measurement, which combined as *geometria,* measurement of land. The story of *algebra* is more complex. The word comes from Arabic *el,* the, and *jabr,* to reunite, which formed *jabara,* to set broken bones, to restore. A mathematician, al-Kwarizmi, gave the word currency in a book title: *Ilm el-jabr wa'l-mukabala,* for a book about equating like and like. From the book the word *algebra* developed as the name for a branch of mathematics but also to designate the surgical treatment of fractures. Although modern schoolchildren may feel fractured by algebra, the old surgical meaning became obsolete in the seventeenth century.

amuck. *Amuck* or *amok*, for what crazed or frantic people may run, is a Malay word, spelled *amoq* or *amok*. In the Malay language it describes a furious and murderous frenzy, but as adopted in English it may describe less vicious loss of control.

apache. *Apache*, as a name for hoodlums or rowdies in Paris, apparently is an example of a word going from America to France. As the name of an American Indian tribe, *Apache* is probably derived from Zuni *apachu*, enemy, and seemed suitable for Paris gangs and for the dance that involves an apache throwing a girl about a stage.

artichoke. The word *choke* has nothing to do with the origin of the name of the vegetable, although the prickly fiber surrounding its heart is sometimes called the choke, on the theory that it's possible to choke by inadvertently eating it. Actually the English name is an adaptation from the name the Arabs gave the vegetable, *alkarshuf*, meaning thistle; the plant looks like a thistle. The word came through Italian *articiocco* and Spanish *alcachofa* to English. *Jerusalem artichoke* is a different vegetable and took the name of the city only through mispronunciation. It is a variation on Italian *girasole articiocco,* sunflower artichoke. The plant is a kind of sunflower, with an edible root.

belfry. There may be bells—or bats—in a belfry, but the origin of the word has nothing to do with them. *Belfry* comes from a Middle English word, *berfrey,* the name for a movable tower used by a besieging army. This goes back to old Germanic words, *bergen,* to protect, plus *frid,* peace. When the name was applied to a church tower, the presence of bells may have influenced the spelling.

belladonna. The poisonous plant, deadly nightshade, and the drug extracted from it took the Italian word for beautiful lady, presumably because the drug was used to enhance a lady's appearance by dilating the pupils of her eyes.

bias. One story attributes the origin of the word *bias* to the name of a weight attached to a bowling ball to make it swerve from a direct course. Actually the word goes back to Old French *biais,* a slope or slant, although it did later become the name of the weight producing a curve in the roll of a bowling ball. The swerve in the course of the ball provides an extra challenge for the bowler.

boondocks. American soldiers in the Philippines during World War II learned the Tagalog word for mountain, *bundok*. They brought the word home, where it generalized to apply to not only mountainous country but any remote or isolated or uncivilized area. "Out in the boondocks" or "boonies" is like "out in the tules."

caper. English acquired *caper* from Latin *caper*, goat, through Italian *capriolare*, to leap or gambol. English *capriole*, for a leap in dancing or a jump by a trained horse, appeared in the sixteenth century. *Caper*, an abbreviation of *capriole*, means to skip about or gambol, and as a noun refers to a prank or in slang to a criminal exploit, especially a robbery. A different *caper* names a prickly Mediterranean bush whose green flower buds are pickled and used for flavoring.

chap. *Chap*, sometimes spelled *chop*, has a variety of meanings in English, derived from different roots. Going back to Old Norse, *chap* or *chop* can refer to the jaw or cheek, which accounts for *chapfallen*, meaning depressed or disheartened, and for "licking one's chops." A different word, Old English *ceap*, meant trade or bargain, and produced *cheap* and *cheapen* in English, related to German *kaufen*, to buy or purchase. It also produced *chapman* in Old English, for a trader or peddler, and later *chapbook*, for books sold by chapmen. *Chapman* was shortened in modern English to just *chap* and generalized to mean a fellow or man. Going back to French *couper*, to cut, English developed *chop*, to cut, usually with short blows of an axe or cleaver, and *chop* as the name for the piece of meat produced by a chop. This specialized to *chap* to refer to a split or crack in the skin. *Chaps* for the heavy protective leather worn by cowboys is a still different word, a shortening of Spanish *chaparejos*.

coleslaw. The name for a cabbage salad combines Dutch *kool,* a cabbage, which comes from Latin *caulis,* and Dutch *sla,* salad. The more recent shift to *cold slaw* results from mistaken pronunciation and recognition that the salad is served cold. The new erroneous spelling also gives us *hot slaw.*

coon. *Raccoon,* for the native American tree-climbing animal with black masklike markings across its eyes, comes from Algonquian *arakunem,* one who scratches with the hands. The word was abbreviated in America to *coon* early in the eighteenth century and developed various applications to people. In one specific use it was applied to a Whig because in 1840 the party used a picture of a raccoon as its emblem. It also designated a loutish white man. Toward the end of the nineteenth century it became an offensive term for a black person, gaining wide currency especially from an 1896 song by Ernest Hogan, "All *Coons* Look Alike to Me." With the tendency of usage to avoid racially insulting terms, the use has almost disappeared, and terms like *coon dog* and *coon hunt* can be used with their literal meaning, referring to hunting raccoons.

coquette. Old French *coq*, cock, inspired *coqueter*, to strut like a rooster; and English adopted *coquet* as a verb meaning to flirt. Spanish derived *coquetear*, to flirt. Samuel Johnson's eighteenth-century dictionary defines it "to entertain with compliments and amorous tattle." As a noun *coquet* could refer to either sex, but when the French feminine form, *coquette*, was adopted, the word was applied only to women who trifle with men's affections.

corduroy. *Corduroy* has long been associated with French *corde du roi*, the king's cord, perhaps to give the cloth a little prestige. But the French phrase doesn't appear in the French language, and it seems likely that *corduroy* is a combination of *cord* and obsolete *duroy*, the name of a coarse cloth once produced in England. That is, corduroy is corded duroy. Corduroy roads, which looked as if they were corded like the cloth, were built in nineteenth-century America, made of logs laid crosswise on the roadbed.

cravat. *Cravate* is the French name for a Croation. The scarves worn by Croation soldiers in the seventeenth century were called *cravates* as the French adopted and popularized them, and English adopted the word more generally as a synonym for *necktie*.

curfew. In the Middle Ages a bell rung at a certain time during the evening signaled that people should put out lights, cover fires, and retire. French *couvre feu,* cover fire, named the event and easily became English *curfew.*

debut. French *jouer de but,* to play for a mark or goal, was shortened to *début,* as a term in games to indicate the opening stroke in billiards or the leadoff in bowls. English adopted the word for more general uses, to name various kinds of introductions, of an actor in a first play or a girl entering society. More recently it has become an unpronounceable verb.

doodle. A Turkish *düdük* was a flute, and a Polish *dudy* was a bagpipe, with its name derived from the Turkish. Then German *dudeln* developed, meaning to play the bagpipe. In English the early meaning of *doodle* was to play the bagpipe. A *doodlesack* is a bagpipe. *Doodle* generalized to mean to trifle or dawdle. It also specialized to refer to aimless scribbling or drawing.

easel. *Easel* comes from Dutch *ezel,* a donkey, and apparently reflects some resemblance between the animal and the artist's legged frame; compare *sawhorse.* The French name for an easel is *chavalet,* from *cheval,* horse.

flair. *Flair* started out to denote a keen sense of smell, adopted in Middle English from French *flairer,* to emit an odor, which goes back to Latin *fragrare,* the source of

English *fragrance*. By the late nineteenth century the English word had generalized to suggest any kind of ability at keen discernment, not just a sense of smell, to refer to a knack or aptitude.

garble. A *garbler* was once a British official whose duty was to inspect and sift drugs and spices. His name comes from Arabic *gharbala,* to sift through a sieve, and *garble* meant to sift or sort out. When applied to writings, this sorting or editing could lead to distortion, and the word came to refer mainly to confusion or perversion of a text, especially in a quotation.

garnish. Old French *guarnir* or *warnir* meant to protect or warn or prepare to defend. When it was adopted in English, it extended in two directions. When persons were known to be heavily in debt, other people were warned so that they wouldn't lend them money. The persons warned were called *garnishees.* And then the word developed into a verb, *to garnish* or usually *to garnishee,* to attach property or a salary so that it can be used to discharge a debt. In another direction, *garnish* moved from the meaning of protect to its current sense. When a town was *garnished*, it was fortified; devices for protection were added. *Garnish* generalized to refer to any kind of addition, and to *garnish* is to embellish or decorate or trim, especially to put something like parsley on a plate of food.

geezer. A *geezer* is usually labeled old and is usually a man. The word *geezer* is still frequently classified as slang, but it seems to be in wide use. It comes from *guise*, a word that comes from Old High German and French *wisa*, meaning customary behavior or manner. *Guise* led to British dialect *guiser* for a person who went from house to house in disguise offering entertainment, a mummer; *geezer* started as a variant of *guiser*. The British music-hall song of 1890, "Knocked 'Em in the Old Kent Road," refers to a "Nice old geezer with a nasty cough." *Guise* now usually refers to a kind of false appearance, as in "under the guise of friendship he betrayed her." *Guise* also led to Old French *desguiser*, to change costume, and English *disguise*, to make appear different.

gourmet. The word that English has adopted to name an epicure, a connoisseur of good food and wine, was used in French as a name for a servant and then for a vintner's assistant, who might be a wine taster. The French word was the origin of English *groom*, closer to the earlier meaning, and also of *gourmand*, originally a glutton but now usually a person much like a gourmet. *Gourmet*, frequently with an anglicized pronunciation to *gormet*, has recently become popular with advertisers as an adjective praising almost any kind of food.

graffiti. *Graffiti* is the plural form of *graffito*, which comes from Italian *graffio*, a scratch. Before the 1960s the term was used mainly by art historians or archeologists and referred to drawings or writing on buildings in ancient Rome or Pompeii. In the 1960s an outburst of drawing or scribbling on walls of public buildings or on New York subway trains gave the word, almost always the plural form only, wide popular use. The Italian probably comes from Latin *graphium*, stylus, and Greek *grapheion*, to write, and is related to *graft* and *graph*. *Graft* may have developed its main meaning, to implant a shoot from one plant into a groove or slot in another in which it continues to grow, from the resemblance of the pointed insert to a stylus. It is unclear how this meaning expanded in America in the nineteenth century to refer to getting money or influence by dishonest means, especially by abusing a position, as in "political graft." In this sense, *graft* was at first considered slang, but currently it is accepted as standard English.

groggy. Admiral Edward Vernon of the Royal Navy always wore a grogram suit. *Grogram* is from Old French *grosgrain*, from *gros*, coarse, and *grain*, and referred to a coarse fabric. From his customary dress, Vernon was known as Old Grog, and when in 1845 he ordered as an economy that rum issued to sailors should be diluted with water, the new unpopular drink was named for him. Still some sailors drank too much of it and were described as groggy. *Groggy* has generalized to refer to any unsteadiness or dizziness, not necessarily intoxication from grog.

gun. In the fourteenth century there is a record that a *ballista*, a device for hurling rocks and other missiles, was called *Gunhild*, a shortened form of a Scandinavian female name Gunnhildr. Both parts of the name, *gunn* and *hildr*, mean war. This seems the best guess for the origin of *gun*, which was apparently applied to devices like catapults as well as weapons using gunpowder. One of these early machines for throwing stones was called a *mangonne*, and another guess assumes that *gonne* was an abbreviation for *mangonne*.

gunnysack. Sanskrit *goni* simply means sack or bag, but it was adapted as *gunny* for a coarse cloth manufactured usually from jute in Bengal.

harass. Accented on either the first or second syllable, *harass* goes back to Old French *harer*, meaning to set a dog on, and to *hare*, the cry used as a command to the dog. The word may be related to *harry*, which comes from Anglo-Saxon *here*, army or host. Both to harass and to harry were originally to raid or plunder an enemy, but the words have come to refer more generally to any kind of tormenting or persistent annoyance. Currently, with greater awareness of problems like stalking and with the enactment of new laws, the word is most often associated with sexual harassment.

harbor. The origin of *harbor* is military. The word goes back to Old High German *herberga,* a combination of *here,* army, plus *berga,* shelter. The word came into English through Anglo-Saxon as *harbor* and shifted emphasis to refer to any refuge or place of safety but especially a protected inlet of the sea. The origin of the word is reflected in its twentieth-century specific use to name a halting place for tanks. From the same source, *harbinger* came into the language in Middle English as a name for a person sent in advance to arrange lodgings for an army. That use became obsolete as the meaning generalized to refer to any herald or forerunner and then figuratively to a sign of a coming event—"a harbinger of spring."

hazard. Arabic *az-zahr* was the name for a die used in gaming. The word came into Spanish as *azar,* meaning chance or risk, and then into Old French as *hasard* and English as *hazard.* There is still a dice game called hazard, but the word more commonly means risk, danger, jeopardy.

isinglass. *Isinglass* has been in the language since the sixteenth century and has come a long way from its origin in Dutch words *huizen,* meaning sturgeon, and *blas,* meaning bladder. *Isinglass,* from a combination of the Dutch words, originally referred to a gelatin made from the internal membranes of fish bladders, used in cooking and also in making glue. As early as the seventeenth century, the name was applied to thin sheets of mica, which looked like the transparent gelatin and could be used in various kinds of windows. In the musical *Oklahoma,* the surrey with the fringe on top had "isinglass curtains you can roll right down, in case there's a change in the weather."

jaunty. The origin of *jaunt* is obscure, although in one of its meanings *jaunt* refers to the felly or rim of a wheel and is from Old French *jante.* In Ireland a jaunting car is a two-wheeled cart with seats arranged back-to-back on each side. *Jaunty,* however, has nothing to do with *jaunt* or short trips, but comes from French *gentil,* genteel or gentle. It originally meant well bred or gentlemanly, but has shifted to mean perky or carefree: "He wore his hat at a jaunty angle."

jerky. The name for the jerky or jerked beef or venison that was a staple in the early American West had nothing to do with the common word *jerk.* It is a corruption of Spanish *charqui,* meaning dried and cut.

journey. Latin *dies*, day, went through some sound changes to become French *journée* and then became the basis of a number of English words. A *journey* was the distance to be traveled in a day, generalized later to refer to any travel from one place to another, a trip. A *journal* is a daily record—a *diary*, which comes from *dies* without going through French—but the meaning of *journalism* has expanded to refer to any newspaper work. A *journeyman* was once a day laborer. A *sojourn* is a brief visit, although now it may last longer than a day.

jubilee. Hebrew *yobel* was the name for a ram or a ram's horn. According to the Book of Leviticus in the Bible, a ram's horn, the "trumpet of the jubile," was to be sounded on the day of atonement. English *jubilee* descended from the name for the ram's horn, influenced by Latin *jubilum*, a wild shout.

juke. *Juke* or *joog*, of African origin, occurs in the Gullah dialect of islanders off the South Carolina and Georgia coasts. It means disorderly or wicked. *Juke joint* retains some of that earlier meaning; a *jukebox*, although it may seem loud or even disorderly, is not considered wicked.

julep. A mint julep may be associated with the American South, but its name goes back to Persian. Persian *gul,* rose, combined with *ab,* water, to produce *gulab,* rose water.

junket. Latin *juncus,* rush, was the source of French *jonquette,* for a basket made of rushes used to carry sweetmeats or cream cheese to market. In Italian the delicacy carried in the rush basket was called *giuncata,* which produced English *junket,* referring especially to a confection of milk sweetened and thickened. The meaning of *junket* expanded to refer to a feast or a picnic. Then in nineteenth-century America the word extended still further from the basket made of rushes to refer to a trip or journey, especially a trip taken by an official at public expense.

ketchup. The Chinese word *ke-tsiap* and the Malay word *kechap* both originally meant taste. Another Chinese word *k'e chap* means tomato juice. All of these may be behind English *ketchup,* also spelled *catsup* or *catchup.*

lunch. Spanish *lonja,* a slice of ham, is apparently behind a North England dialect word, *lounge,* for a hunk of bread and cheese, and also English *lunch.*

lung. The respiratory organ of most vertebrates gets its name from its weight. The word *lung* derives ultimately from an Indo-European word meaning light in weight, which is the origin also of the word *lights* to refer to the lungs, especially of cattle or sheep when the organ is used as food.

magazine. The Arabic word *makhẓan* was a name for a storehouse or granary. English *magaẓine* came from it and keeps the earlier sense in its use for a military supply depot or a storage space for explosives or the space in a pistol or rifle that holds cartridges. The word developed its most common use today as a storehouse for written material, used once for a book but now usually only for a periodical. French *magasin*, a department store, also came from *makhẓan*.

mohair. The Arabic word *mokhayyer* was the name of a kind of cloth made from the hair of Angora goats. When the cloth, or an imitation of it, was introduced in England in the sixteenth century, the name didn't make sense and the English altered it to *mohair*, apparently since the cloth looked like hair. But a century later a different kind of cloth, with a watery or wavelike appearance, usually silk, took its name from French *mouaire*, for *mohair*, and was called *moire*. The use of *moire* as the name for the wavelike cloth was reinforced by French *moirer*, to water.

muddle. *Mud* and *muddle* are related to Dutch *modden*, meaning to dabble in mud. *Muddle* in a now obsolete sense meant to bathe or wallow in mud or muddy water. By extension *to muddle* is to mix ingredients for a drink or to fuddle or confuse with an alcoholic drink or generally to make things murky or cloudy. Followed by *through*, *to muddle* is to work in a haphazard or ineffective manner but still manage to succeed.

negligee. English adapted *negligee* from French *négliger*, to neglect, and it first applied generally to casual or unceremonious dress of any sort, perhaps as if propriety were neglected. It is now most often applied to a woman's dressing gown, which may not neglect design or style or cost. The French accent mark in *negligee* has been abandoned in modern dictionaries.

phony. From Irish *fainne*, a ring, British slang in the late eighteenth century developed *fawney*, a ring. Grose's 1796 *Dictionary of the Vulgar Tongue* defines *fawney-dropping* or *fawney rig* (Grose defines *rig* as "fun, game, diversion, or trick"): "A fellow drops a brass ring, double gilt, which he picks up before the party meant to be cheated, and to whom he disposes of it for less than its supposed, and ten times more than its real, value." Money droppers practiced a variation on the scam. The swindler drops counterfeit money in front of a "flat," a dupe or greenhorn, and gets good change for it. The best guess seems to be that *phony*, not genuine, fake, which was common in America by 1900, was derived from *fawney* and its association with deception. Other guesses derive the word from *telephone*. Another theory derives the word from *Forney rings* circulated by street peddlers and manufactured by a man named Forney.

poke. At least three different words spelled *poke* exist in English, and all of them have developed a variety of uses. One of them came from Algonquin *apooke*, tobacco, and is the name for various plants, wild tobacco, and pokeweed. The most common *poke* came from Dutch *poken* and means to push or prod or jab, with many variations. You can poke your nose into somebody's affairs, poke the fire with a poker, poke around aimlessly, or poke along lazily, dawdling, being a slowpoke. Another *poke* is from Old French *poque* or *poche*, bag or sack. *Poke* as a name for a sack is now mainly a dialect form, although it survives in "pig in a poke," something you acquire sight unseen. *Pouch* has the same origin in Old French, and *poach* comes from an Old French variant, *pochier*, meaning to enclose in a bag. A *poached egg* involves cooking the yolk in a pocket of white. It's uncertain which meaning of *poke* was adopted to name a *poke bonnet*, with a projecting front bill, called a *poke*. *Cowpoke*, like *cowprodder* and *cowpuncher*, presumably refers to what a cowboy does to cows.

punch. The Hindi word *panch*, five, is used for various kinds of mixtures of five ingredients, sauces or foods or a medical preparation made from sprouts of five different trees. English adopted the word for a sweet drink that originally had five ingredients, specified in one recipe as arrack, lemon, tea, sugar, and water. *Punch-drunk*, however, has nothing to do with drinking too much punch, but comes from the verb *punch*, to strike with the fist, and originally designated a boxer punched to dizziness.

rake. In its most common sense, to indicate what a gardener does to leaves in the fall or the tool he uses, *rake* has a straightforward origin, from Anglo-Saxon *raca* and Old Norse *reka*, a spade. But in the sixteenth century the word *rakehell* was coined, presumably from the notion that it referred to something so evil that you had to rake hell to find it. And that was shortened to *rake* to refer to a roué, a high-living or dissolute person. A different word *rake* was apparently a Scandinavian sea term meaning to slant or incline, and so a hat can be worn at a *rakish* angle.

sassafras. The name for the aromatic tree, native to the eastern United States, has an uncertain origin. It apparently came from Spanish *sasafras* and may go back to Latin *saxifraga*, composed from *saxum*, rock, and *frangere*, to break, as the name for a plant that grows in crevices in rock. There is also a theory that it comes from a Narragansett Indian word, *asauakapamuch*. Sass tea, made from the tree's dried roots, is still a spring tonic in some parts of America, alleged to thin the blood.

saunter. Holy land, *sainte terre* in French, is the basis of one of several dubious speculations about the origin of *saunter*. The notion is that people wandering about idly or begging said they were going "à la sainte terre," which became *saunter*. Equally implausible is the explanation that *saunter* comes from French *sans terre*, without land, applied to wanderers without a home. The most plausible theory derives the word from Old French *s'aventurer*, to risk oneself, which produced Middle English *saunter en*, but the "origin obscure" of several dictionaries is also plausible.

scoop. The word *scoop* goes back to a Dutch word for a vessel to bail water or a shovel and has developed in a variety of ways. In America, as a verb, it came to mean vanquish or take advantage of. In poker, for example, it referred to winning, perhaps from the notion of scooping up the chips at the end of a hand. Newspaper usage applied this sense to being first to print a story, scooping the opposition papers. And a newspaper scoop has broadened to refer to any important or new information: "What's the scoop?"

seersucker. The Persian phrase *shir o shakkar* means milk and sugar, and was behind the Hindi *shirshaker*, the name for a crinkled, striped cloth originally imported from India.

skit. *Skit,* for a short, usually comic, theatrical sketch, goes back to Old Norse *skjora*, to shoot, related to English *shoot*. *Skit* can also refer to any kind of verbal shot or satirical comment.

thug. Sanskrit *sthaga*, a cheat or swindler, produced Hindustani *thag*, which produced *thug*, the name applied to an allegedly religious cult in the nineteenth century whose members were less interested in the honor of their goddess Kali than in the profits of thievery and murder. Similarities in behavior made it easy to transfer the name to modern gangsters.

tules. Especially in the American West, *tules* refers to any remote area, the boondocks, or the sticks. It acquired the meaning by generalization from Spanish *tule*, from a Nahuatl word *tollin* or *tullin*, to name a reed or bulrush. The word still keeps its original meaning, referring to various kinds of reeds and rushes or to an area overgrown by tules. But the generalized meaning is more common: "He's out in the tules."

woodchuck. The origin of *woodchuck* has nothing to do with how much wood a woodchuck can chuck. It comes from *otchek*, the Algonquian name for the animal. The woodchuck uses its other name when it acts as a weather prophet on Groundhog Day.

Yankee. *Yankee* is probably the closest the language

comes to providing a general name for a resident of the United States, a name like *Canadian* or *Mexican;* but nobody really knows where the word came from. The most likely guess associates the word with Dutch *Janke,* a diminutive of the common Dutch name Jan. Apparently *Yankee* was used as a nickname for Dutch traders in New England. But how the word shifted to be applied to New Englanders remains a mystery. During the Civil War the word became a term of disparagement, applied to people of the North. Much of this connotation persists in the South of the United States, and *Yankee* is frequently a term of disparagement outside the country—"Yankee go home."

zest. French *ʒeste* names the partition membrane in a nut or orange. English borrowed the word in the fifteenth century to refer to a piece of lemon or orange peel used to add flavor to a drink. The word still sometimes has its early meaning, but more commonly it refers generally to enthusiasm or gusto, as in "a zest for life."

CHAPTER 5

Gods and Legends

MYTHS AND LEGENDS FROM ANCIENT RELI-gions to a modern comic strip—for the origin of *jeep* and *goon*—have been the sources of many words in English. Classical mythology has perhaps been the most obvious contributor to the English vocabu-lary—for example, *chaos* from Greek *chaino,* to gape or yawn, a vast dark void as the "power" in the mythological universe. The classical gods and goddesses, with both their Greek and Latin names, inspired *jovial* from Jove, *martial* from Mars, *venereal* from Venus, *aphrodisiac* from

Aphrodite, *titanic* from the Titans. *Panic* reflects the fear inspired by the god Pan, especially noted for pursuing young nymphs in the forest. The word *pander* comes indirectly from classical mythology. It comes from *Pandarus,* the name of a character who is a procurer or go-between in Chaucer's version of the story of Troilus and Cressida. A Delaware Indian chief, Tamanend, achieved legendary status, partly humorous, as Saint Tammany and is behind the word *Tammany,* the name of the New York political organization. *Immolate,* sacrifice, goes back to ancient religious legend; it comes from Latin *mola,* meal, and refers to the practice of sprinkling meal on a sacrificial lamb. An imaginary Moslem deity, Tervagant, became a character in English morality plays and the basis for *termagant,* for a scolding woman, a shrew.

apple of the eye. The Old English word *æppel* meant fruit but also eyeball or anything round. The word developed in English to name the golden fruit in Greek mythology given by Paris to Aphrodite to get her help in capturing the beautiful Helen and also to name whatever Eve gave Adam to eat in the Garden of Eden. Presumably some of Eve's offering stuck when Adam swallowed, and the projection in the front of the human throat became an *Adam's apple.* The Old English word, however, also retained its meaning as eyeball or pupil of the eye. *The apple of one's eye* refers to the pupil, thought of as the most important part of the eye and by extension to anything precious or cherished. When, as the Old Testament reports, Moses says that God found Jacob in a desert land and "kept him as the apple of his eye," he is using the phrase in its extended sense, to refer to Jacob as the person most cherished.

atlas. Ancient Greek legends identified Atlas in various ways, as a giant compelled to support the world on his shoulders, as a demigod in charge of the pillars holding the world, as a man chained to a mountain with the heavens resting on it. All of these supported the development of the name *Atlas* as a symbol of great strength and inspired the picture, conventional in school geography books, of Atlas with a globe resting on his shoulders. In 1595, a Flemish geographer, Gerhardus Mercator, used this picture on the title page of a collection of maps, *Atlas; or, A Geographical Description of the World*. Atlas's name continued to be associated with a collection of maps and then became a common noun for a collection of data on any subject.

augury. Latin *augere*, to increase, is the source of Latin *augur*, the name for a priest in Rome who foretold the future by examining the entrails of animals or observing the flights of birds. Modern augury, prophecy or soothsaying, still may rely on signs or omens. *Augere,* to increase, also produced other words in English, *augment,* to enlarge or supplement, and *auction,* a sale in which successive bids increase an item's price. Another Latin name for a priest was *auspex,* formed from *avis,* bird, plus *spicere,* to see. This priest saw the future in the flights of birds, and *auspex* is the source of English *auspicious,* of good omen, favorable. It is also the source of English *auspice,* an omen, usually used in the plural with an extended meaning as *auspices,* patronage or protection.

calliope. The name of the Muse of epic poetry, *Kalliope,* means beautiful voice. Her name, ironically, now designates the raucous steam-driven instrument that used to provide the last sound of a circus parade and still howls on Mississippi River boats.

cereal. The Roman goddess Ceres, Demeter to the Greeks, was patroness of farmers and goddess of agriculture. Her name was first used to refer to any edible grains, but in the nineteenth century it became associated specifically with the foods that have come to dominate American breakfasts.

colossal. Latin *colossus* meant gigantic, especially a gigantic statue. The best-known example was the Colossus of Rhodes, a hundred-foot-tall bronze statue of Apollo that stood astride the harbor of the island of Rhodes, one of the seven wonders of the ancient world. *Colossal* originally meant huge or gigantic, like the Colossus, but more recent figurative usage, especially in Hollywood, has made the word a relatively vague term of approval, especially for a film involving many extras in a costly production. *Coliseum* is also derived from *colossus*.

cynosure. Greek *kynikos*, like a dog, is the origin of *cynic*. *Kynosoura*, a dog's tail, according to one legend, produced the name of a nymph, Cynosura, who was placed in the heavens as a star and gave her name to Polaris or the North Star. A more likely explanation is that the Greeks thought of a dog's tail as a likely description of the constellation Ursa Minor and used *Cynosura*, from *kynosoura*, as a name for its main star. The name produced the English word *cynosure* for anything that guides or directs, as the North Star does, or for any center of attention or interest.

disaster. The stars had central importance in many ancient societies, and there are still *astrologers*, from Greek *astron*, star, plus *logos*, knowledge. All sorts of misfortunes could be blamed on the stars, ill-starred events or star-crossed lovers or a disaster, when the stars are against. *Disaster* comes from Latin *dis-*, against, and *astrum*, star. *Consider* and *desire* come from a different Latin word for star, *sidus, sideris*. *To consider* was to consult with the stars, *to desire* was to await and wish for something from the stars.

earwig. A persistent zoological myth is responsible for the name of the unattractive but durable insect common in gardens. Probably from their nocturnal habits, the superstition developed that the insects crawled into ears and thence into brains. The name combined *ear* with Anglo-Saxon *wicga,* meaning beetle or worm, but there is no evidence that earwigs have ever had any special interest in ears.

erotic. Greek Eros, called Cupid by the Romans, was a god of love, who in some early legends preceded all the other gods as the force necessary to create them. Later writers changed his nature, making him a slightly mischievous child-god, given to shooting golden arrows to inspire love or lead arrows to destroy love. English *erotic,* causing sexual feelings, derives from *Eros,* and its synonym, *amatory,* from one of his Roman names, Amor. The god's other Latin name came from *cupido,* desire, and English *cupidity* reflects a different aspect of the god's character, suggesting greed, especially a desire for wealth.

hell. In Old Norse mythology Loki's daughter, goddess of death and the underworld, was Hel. Anglo-Saxon *helan* meant to cover or hide. Middle English *helle* was probably influenced by both words and became the biblical hell, also Sheol and Hades. In Christianity it is the place where sinners and fallen angels or devils are punished after death. The word *hell* has also developed a wide variety of figurative and generalized uses. It is an interjection expressing anger or irritation, "Oh, hell," considered at least mildly profane. It has various uses as a general intensive, "Hell no," "a hell of a note." It is an all-purpose metaphor; one can be hot or cold or hungry or tired as hell. Combined with *ion* it produced *hellion,* a troublemaker or person fond of deviltry. One can raise hell and all hell can break loose and there can be hell to pay. *Hell's bells* is rhyming slang. *Hell for leather* as Kipling used it to describe reckless horseback riding may have developed from "all of a lather."

hokum. The word for crude comedy or mawkish sentimentality or just nonsense or bunk ultimately goes back to religious ceremony. *Hokum* originated as American slang as an alteration of *hocus,* to trick or hoax, which is an abbreviation of *hocus pocus,* meaningless words used as a formula by magicians or conjurers. *Hocus pocus,* however, is a pseudo-Latin, not totally respectful, variation on the form for a sacramental blessing, *hoc est corpus,* this is the body.

humor. When *humor* came into Middle English, it had nothing to do with comedy or being funny. It came from

Latin *humor*, moisture, and was an important term in an elaborate picture of the universe, a system of order that persisted into the seventeenth century. The universe was composed of four elements—earth, air, fire, and water—and human beings contained four corresponding fluids: blood, phlegm, yellow bile, and black bile. These were called humors. The balance of these fluids determined the temperament of an individual; too much blood, for example, made one sanguine. *Sanguis* is the Latin word for blood. The early meaning persists in expressions like "She's in a foul humor this morning" or in the verb *to humor*, meaning to indulge or make allowances for some kind of behavior. Any disproportion in humors could be used to account for eccentricities in behavior, and in Shakespeare's time playwrights were exploiting the theory. Ben Jonson created the "comedy of humors," in which characters obsessed with qualities like jealousy or greed created what is now called humor. In the prologue to *Every Man in His Humour*, Jonson defines his intent to "sport with human follies" that could be laughed at. The use of *humor* to describe the quality that makes something seem funny, amusing, or ludicrous was established in the late sixteenth century. Earlier meanings of *humor* persist behind modern connotations of the term as distinguished, perhaps, from *wit*. A distinction is sometimes made describing humor as an expression of incongruities or peculiarities in a character or situation, often genial or kindly, whereas wit is primarily intellectual, likely to be sharp and biting. *Black humor* is a term that has developed recently to exploit the paradox of a comedy based on unpleasant or even tragic situations.

inaugurate. In ancient Rome *augurs* foretold events by interpreting omens, such as the flight of birds or the appearance of the entrails of sacrificial animals. English adopted *augur* and also created *augury* to mean an omen or sign or portent. In Rome officials were installed only after approval from augurs, and Latin created the word *inaugurare,* meaning to consecrate by augury. Presidents are now inaugurated without approval from the entrails of animals.

jeep. In 1936 E. C. Segar's comic strip, "Popeye, the Sailor," which had already contributed the word *goon* to the language, introduced a new character, Eugene the Jeep, a small animal with supernatural powers. The name caught on and was applied in various ways—to an army recruit, to an ill-fitting coat or hat, to an autogiro as a *jumping jeep.* The comic strip was popular in the army, and GI's applied *jeep* to the new all-purpose army vehicles, perhaps partly because the cars were labeled *GP,* for General Purpose. This application stuck, and *jeep* became the official name for the vehicle in Europe as well as America.

juggernaut. *Juggernaut* now seems mainly useful figuratively, for example, as a sportswriter's word to describe a crushing line on a football team or in England as the name for a large heavy truck, but the word has specific significance in Hindu mythology. It comes from Sanskrit *Jagannatha,* from *jagat,* world, plus *natha,* lord, which meant lord of the world, and was a name applied to an incarnation of the god Vishnu. The idol of the god, which was pulled through the streets for religious ceremonies, acquired frightening forms in some legends, tall with sixteen huge wheels. And supposedly worshipers in their zeal threw themselves under the wheels and were crushed. Figuratively *juggernaut* now refers to any terrible force or anything exacting blind devotion or sacrifice.

lullaby. In some Jewish mythology Lilith was the first wife of Adam. She refused to submit to Adam and left Paradise to become an evil spirit. Coins with pictures of Adam and Eve and the words "Avaunt thee Lilith" were used as protections. And *lullaby* was said to be derived from *Lilla, abi,* Lillith avaunt. This is a curious example of folk etymology; the actual origin of the word is much simpler. *Lull* was a Middle English word, probably from Dutch *lollen,* to sing, related to Latin *lallare,* to sing to sleep. The word apparently originated as imitation of sounds like *la* in singing a baby to sleep. Addition of the meaningless *by* produced *lullaby*.

lunatic. Long-standing superstitions and fantasies connect the moon with various kinds of behavior. Werewolves react to the full moon as do lovers afflicted with moonlight madness. Dogs are thought to howl at the moon. In old superstitions madness was linked to the moon, with changes in violence related to the moon's phases. As a result English developed the word *lunatic*, from Latin *luna*, the moon. Its slang version, *luny* or *loony*, may echo *loon*, the name of the bird whose weird cry inspires the phrase "crazy as a loon."

maudlin. Mary Magdalene, whom Christ freed from evil spirits, was represented by medieval painters with eyes red and swollen from weeping. English pronunciation changed her name to *maudlin*, to mean foolishly and tearfully sentimental.

meander. The river Maiandros in ancient Phrygia was noted for its wandering course. Latin picked up the name as *maeander*, and English adopted it as a geological term to describe broad swinging curves made by a river on its floodplain. *Meander* generalized in English as a verb. A stream may meander by taking a winding or tortuous course, or a person may meander by rambling aimlessly through the woods or by wandering idly through thoughts.

mistletoe. The parasitic plant with yellowish-green flowers and white berries in winter has been endowed with mystic powers since the time of the Druids, in modern times especially as a Christmas decoration promoting romance. But the origin of the name is not romantic. *Mistle* in Old English was the name for bird lime, the sticky substance spread on twigs to catch birds. It was related to Old Danish *mest*, meaning dung. *Mistle* combined with Old English *tan*, meaning twig, to form *mistaletan*, altered to *mistletoe* when *tan* disappeared as a word. The name reflects a popular notion that the plant sprang from bird droppings, a tradition going back at least to Pliny. It is interesting that Sir Thomas Browne in *Pseudoxia Epidemica; or, Vulgar Errors* (1646) has a learned discussion to expose the error in the notion that "mistletoe is bred upon trees, from seeds which birds let fall thereon."

morphine. Greek *morphe*, meaning form, provides a suffix in a number of English words, but it also produced the name of the Greek god of dreams, *Morpheus*, referring to the forms seen in dreams. The drug *morphine* was named for Morpheus, partly because of an assumption by some English poets that he was also the god of sleep.

music. The nine Muses danced and sang on Mount Helicon and Mount Parnassus, and various English words echo their activities. The arts they practiced were called *mousike*; the word specialized to refer to the making of pleasant sounds and through Latin *musica* and French *musique* became English *music*. *Mouseion* was the Greek name for a temple or haunt of the Muses, and English *museum* is derived from it.

pants. The most recent edition of the *Oxford English Dictionary* has dropped its designation of pants as "a vulgar abbrev. of pantaloons—chiefly U.S." The change seems appropriate, since the word goes back to the name of a saint, Saint Pantelone, the patron saint of Venice. The saint's name was adopted for a stock character in early Italian comedy, a slender, foolish old man who wore over his long legs trousers that extended to his feet. The word *pantaloon* came into English by the sixteenth century as a name for an old man, and then to refer to his costume. Clipped to *pants* it became, at least in America, a standard synonym for *trousers*.

pariah. *Pariah* has generalized in English to refer to any social outcast, a pariah dog or a person rejected by others. In Tamil, the language of a people of southern India and northern Sri Lanka, *aparai* was a large drum beaten at certain festivals. A *paraiyar* was a drummer. Drummers were apparently not held in high regard, and *pariah* became the name for a member of a low Hindu caste in southern India, frequently one employed as a servant by the English.

peony. The root of the peony was in ancient times regarded as a charm and also as effective medicine. It was named for Apollo, also called Paion, whose duties included acting as physician of the gods. The name is also the source of the word *paean*, which in ancient Greece designated a hymn of thanksgiving, especially to Apollo. *Paean* now refers to any song of joy or triumph.

pontificate. Latin *pontiff*, derived from words meaning to make sacrificial offerings, designated a high priest. It has come to refer mainly to the Roman Catholic pope. The verb *pontificate* was formed from *pontiff*, and originally it meant to officiate or function as a pontiff. More often today it has degenerated and means to speak pompously or dogmatically or both.

saturnine. The Roman god Saturn, in spite of a shady background—he castrated his father and ate his children—was worshiped as the god of the harvest. An annual weeklong feast was named for him, Saturnalia. *Saturnine*, however, was not derived directly from the name of the god. Ancient astronomers named a planet for him, the sixth in order from the sun. Astrologers used the word *saturnine* for persons born under the sign of this distant planet, characterizing them as cold, sluggish, gloomy, heavy, morose.

shamrock. *Seamar* is the Irish word for clover, and *seamrog*, its diminutive, is behind modern *shamrock*. According to tradition, Saint Patrick used the shamrock with its three leaves to symbolize the Trinity, and it became the national symbol of Ireland.

shibboleth. We use the word *shibboleth*, a Hebrew word that could refer to either an ear of corn or a stream or flood, as a password or any sign or symbol to distinguish a group. Its current use stems from a biblical tale. The Gileadites defeated the Ephraimites in a battle but had trouble distinguishing the fleeing Ephraimites from their own men. Jephthah, one of the judges of Israel, hit on a device for identification. According to Judges 12:5–6, a captain would call the suspected spy into his tent. He would ask, "Art thou an Ephraimite? If he said, Nay: Then said they unto him, Say now Shibboleth: and he said Sibboleth: for he could not frame to pronounce it right. Then they took him, and slew him at the passage of the Jordan." In World War II, American soldiers used the same device to expose Japanese posing as Chinese, asking them to pronounce words like *lily* or *lollipop* because Japanese usually give *l* the sound of *r*.

sticks. The origin of *sticks* is interesting because the word is sometimes explained by an ingenious exercise in folk etymology. This explanation relies on the similar sounds of *sticks* and *Styx,* the mythical river in Hades that souls had to cross. The notion is that Styx came to symbolize any remote place, and popular speech began talking of the backcountry or unsophisticated places as the sticks. Actually the origin of *sticks* as a term for rural districts, in show business for any place outside New York, is neither very complicated nor very glamorous. *Stick* was used as early as the eighteenth century in England to refer to timber. It was used occasionally to refer to a grove of trees in America in the nineteenth century, and a Canadian book, *Black Canyon* (1857), includes the following bit of dialogue: "Before sun up you whitemen go. Go back in the stick (forests far, far, far)." Similar uses early in this century show the word generalizing to refer to any backwoods or rural area.

syringe. Syrinx was a water nymph in classical mythology, much admired by Pan, who chased her, finally caught her on the banks of the river Ladon, and embraced her, only to have her transformed, to save her virtue, into a bundle of reeds. Pan's desire persisted, and to keep the nymph with him he joined a row of the reeds as pipes on which he could play. The pipe was called a *syrinx* in Greek, and the word came to refer to anything tubular or pipe shaped. Through Latin *syringa* the word produced English *syringe* for a device fitted at one end with a rubber bulb by means of which a fluid can be drawn in and ejected. *Syrinx* is also behind the name of the common shrub syringa or mock orange, perhaps from the use of the plants to make pipes or pipe stems.

tantalize. Various legends describe how Tantalus, a Lydian king and a son of Zeus, overreached his status and tried to act like a god. In one legend he invited the gods to dinner and served his son Pelops in a stew. The gods were not fooled, were offended, refused to eat, pulled the dismembered Pelops out of the broth and restored him to life, and devised as a punishment for Tantalus that he should be eternally hungry and thirsty but unable to reach the water around him or the fruit that hung just out of his reach. *Tantalize*, tease, commemorates his punishment.

venereal. Venus was the Roman goddess of love, and *venus* was a Latin word for love. The reputation of the goddess is suggested in the development of the word *venereal*, emphasizing sexual love and referring specifically to diseases transmitted through sexual intercourse. A different attitude toward Venus produced a development in a different direction. Latin *venerari*, to worship, from *venus*, is the root of English *venerate*, to worship or look on with respect. With still another emphasis, *venus* produced Latin *venenum*, originally a love potion or charm and later a drug or poison, and ultimately English *venom*, the poison secreted by some snakes, and then, by generalization, spite or malice. *Revere*, however, a synonym of *venerate*, comes from a different Latin root, *vereri*, to fear or be in awe of. With her Greek name *Aphrodite*, the goddess inspired English *aphrodisiac*, a drug or anything else arousing sexual desire.

venery. English has two *venery*s. One from Roman Venus, goddess of love, means sexual intercourse or indulgence. The other is from Latin *venari*, to hunt, and refers to hunting or the chase. An extensive list of "terms of venery" grew up in the early Renaissance in England as part of the rituals of hunting. *The Book of St. Albans* (1486) collected the terms and is the source for James Lipton's 1968 book *An Exaltation of Larks; or, The Venereal Game*. The list of terms includes many that are still familiar and used to be taught in elementary school: *a pride of lions, a gaggle of geese, a host of angels*. Less well known are *a pod of seals, a rafter of turkeys, a gam of whales, a mur-*

der of crows. Lipton suggests that the creation of new terms is an amusing word game: *a flush of plumbers, an unction of undertakers, a blare of strumpets.*

volcano. The Greek Haephestos, god of fire and the blacksmith who fashioned thunderbolts for Zeus, was called Vulcan by the Romans. The word *volcano* is a natural derivative, as are *vulcanize* and *vulcanite,* both of which involve treating rubber with heat.

CHAPTER 6

Proper Nouns to Common

ANY PEOPLE AND PLACES ARE LONG FOR-
gotten except for their survival as the sources
of English words. A French general and drill
master, J. Martinet, has no place in history except that his
methods of conducting drills inspired the word *martinet*.
A. J. Sax invented important designs for musical instru-
ments but is remembered mostly for the saxophone,
which was named for him. John Philip Sousa is remembered as the march king but also for an instrument used in
marching bands, the *sousaphone*. *Masochism* comes from

Leopold von Sacher-Masoch, an Austrian writer; *sadism* from Count Donatien de Sade, whose eighteenth-century writings describe various sexual aberrations; *dunce* from John Duns Scotus, whose followers in the fourteenth cen-tury were called *Dunsmen,* then *Dunses,* and were regarded as foes of Renaissance humanism. *Poinsettia* comes from J. R. Poinsett, an American ambassador to Mexico; *wisteria* comes from an American anatomist, Casper Wistar. Other words come from place-names. *Solecism,* a violation of the conventional usage of a language, comes from the name of the Greek colony Soloi in Cilicia, across the Mediterranean from Athens. The colonists developed their own dialect, which varied from that of Athens, and the Athenians created the word *soloikos,* to describe their transgressions. *Limousine,* literally a hood in French, was named after a costume worn in Limousin. *Tabasco* sauce took its name from the Tabasco River in Mexico.

argosy. Dubrovnik, on the east coast of the Adriatic, was an early center of commerce and culture. The Italian name for the city in the sixteenth century was Ragusa, and a ship sailing from the port was called a *ragusa.* In England the spelling for the port name was modified to *Aragouse* and the term for a ship to *aragusa.* The term generalized to refer to any large merchant vessel, especially one with a valuable cargo, and then to a fleet of such ships, and became the modern word *argosy*. The name of the ship in which Jason set out to find the golden fleece, the Argo, may have influenced the English shift in spelling. But there is also a port in Sicily called Ragusa, and the *Oxford Dictionary of Etymology* suggests that this port rather than early Dubrovnik gave its name to merchant ships and is the source of *argosy*.

ballyhoo. *Bally* is an Irish word for town or village, and Ballyhoo is a town in County Cork. Supposedly the residents of the town were noted for the violence of their debates and were responsible for the English word *bally-hoo*. This is the most common explanation for the origin of the word, but it seems to me not very convincing. The English word does not refer to debate or a general fuss, but to publicity, especially the spiel of a sideshow barker. Other explanations, however, seem not much better. For example, there is a proposal that the word comes from the cry of dervishes in the Oriental Village in the Chicago World's Fair of 1893—*b'Alla hoo*, meaning through God it is. As another dubious explanation, *Harper's Magazine* in 1880 reported a practical joke in which a young man was sent in pursuit of birds "with four wings and two heads" and "the wonderful power of whistling through one bill while they sang through the other." The birds were referred to as ballyhoo birds. The *Oxford English Dictionary* says "origin unknown" and seems to be right.

bloomers. One of the better-known examples of deriving words from proper names, *bloomers* memorializes Amelia Jenks Bloomer, an enthusiastic follower of reformer Susan B. Anthony in the middle of the nineteenth century. Mrs. Bloomer adopted and popularized trousers gathered together at the ankles, and garments named for her became especially popular as costumes for lady bicyclers in the gay '90s. *Bloomer-girl* designated an attractive, perhaps daring young woman of the early twentieth century who might wear bloomers on the beach. Bloomers were still being used in feminine athletics as late as the 1920s; they are not included in most present-day wardrobes.

boycott. Charles Cunningham Boycott, a farmer who acted as the agent for an Irish landlord in County Mayo, set rents that his tenants considered unfair. Under the sponsorship of the Irish Land League, he was ostracized by his neighbors. Shops refused to sell to him, and protesters threatened his property. He fled to England, and the success of the tenants became front-page news. *Boycott,* to refuse to buy or sell or deal with something or someone, became part of the language.

bunk. About 1820 Felix Walker, a member of Congress, made a long, tiresome speech, which some of his colleagues criticized. He protested that the people of his district, which included Buncombe County, South Carolina, wanted him to speak. He said that he was bound "to make a speech for Buncombe." Journalists remembered his words and began calling any long-winded and dull speech *buncombe*—or sometimes *bunkum*, as the spelling for the name of the county was lost. *Bunkum* became standard English for nonsense or twaddle, but shortened to *bunk* it is still considered slang. *Bunk* as the name for a kind of bed is a different word, from Dutch *bank*, a bench or shelf.

chautauqua. *Chautauqua* is a Seneca Indian place-name, supposedly in its base meaning child. According to one legend, when the Senecas first came to the lake that bears the name they encountered a storm so severe that it swept a child into the water. Another legend says that the word means "one has taken out fish there." The name was used for the lake and then a village, and in 1874 a series of summer schools at Chautauqua, New York, was the source for the common noun that describes a type of educational and recreational meeting today, commonly one in which performers impersonate famous characters.

doily. Mr. Doily or Doyley was known in the seventeenth century as a London draper and a "very respectable warehouseman," apparently not important enough for his first name to have survived. But he invented a kind of woolen cloth and also gave his name to the small ornamental napkins called *doilies*.

epicure. The Greek philosopher Epicurus and his followers believed that pleasure was the highest good, but that it was attained by moderation in all things. As the word adopted from his name developed in English, it emphasized the pleasure more than the moderation and indicated a person with a refined taste for food and liquor who likes to indulge it.

faro. The word *faro* came from French *pharaon*, the name given the gambling game because of the picture of an Egyptian Pharoah that appeared on the back of early playing cards.

fletcherize. *Fletcherize* is interesting as an example of words developing from a proper name, having a short popularity, and then almost disappearing from use. The word memorializes dietitian Horace Fletcher, who advocated promoting health by chewing all food until it was thoroughly liquefied: "It's wise to fletcherize." The procedure and the word flourished in the 1920s.

gerrymander. The Massachusetts legislature in 1812, during the governorship of Elbridge Gerry, redistricted the state to serve partisan politics. A newspaper cartoonist observed the strange boundaries of Essex County and produced a map of the county with head and tail to look like a salamander. The name of the creature in the caricature was modified from *salamander* to *gerrymander,* and the word came into the language. To redistrict a state in order to give increased representation to one party is gerrymandering.

gibus. The word *gibus,* with the first syllable pronounced *jib,* is not often used because we don't often see a gibus these days. A *gibus* is the kind of top hat or opera hat that collapses for carrying but can be popped out to its full stature. The inventor, a Parisian named Gibus, gave his name to the hat but did not achieve enough prominence even to get his first name recorded in dictionaries. *Gibbous,* with a hard *g,* is a totally unrelated word, coming from Latin *gibbus,* a hump, meaning rounded, and referring especially to the moon when it is more than half but less than fully illuminated.

guy. In 1605 Guy Fawkes led an attempt to blow up the houses of Parliament as a protest against religious laws of the time, projecting a tunnel from a nearby house into the cellar of the Parliament building. The plot, called the Gunpowder Plot, was discovered the day before an explosion was planned, and Fawkes was captured, tortured, and hanged. The escape of the legislators is still celebrated in England on Guy Fawkes Day, November 5, with Fawkes as a national villain. For a long time the major character in the celebration was an effigy of Guy Fawkes, made of old clothes and stuffed with straw or rags. Children dragged the effigy about, asking for "a penny for the guy." In England *guy* may still designate someone grotesque in appearance, like the effigy, the guy. In America the word has developed differently, partly fulfilling a real need in the language for a neutral word to mean just a person. Although some dictionaries label it slang, it has no derogatory connotations in expressions like "a regular guy" or "a good guy." Colloquially *guy* has become the most common way of simply designating a male: "the guys at the office" or "That's my guy," almost totally replacing words like *fellow* or *chap*. Increasingly the word is also used of females; a waitress asking "What can I get you guys?" may be addressing women, who may be offended by being called guys. American usage seems to ignore *guy*'s unsavory ancestry; whereas *boy* and *girl* are increasingly suspect, partly because of alleged racist and sexist connections, and partly because they are associated with menial positions, suggesting that in America it is worse to be a servant than a traitor.

Hobson's choice. Thomas Hobson or Jobson, who died in 1631, was a livery-stable keeper in Cambridge. He let out his horses only in strict rotation. Each customer was obliged to take the horse nearest the stable door or to take none. *Hobson's choice,* then, is not a choice between alternatives but a choice between what is offered and nothing. This etymology is the kind of interesting story that thrives on frequent repetition, but the expression may actually have antedated the horse lender. Ernest Weekley spots a 1617 comment by one Richard Cock: "We are put to Hodgson's choise to take such privilegese as they will geve us, or else goe without."

hooch. A small Indian tribe on Admiralty Island, Alaska, took their name from *hutsnuwu,* a grizzly bear fort, and were called *Hoochinoo* or *Hootzenoo* Indians. In the late nineteenth century soldiers in Alaska found that the tribe produced a kind of whiskey, which the soldiers called *hoochinoo,* from the name of the tribe. During Prohibition the hoochinoo began appearing in towns in the American Northwest, and its name, shortened to *hooch,* spread as slang throughout the country. The name of the dance called *hootchy-kootchy* developed with no apparent relation to *hooch.* The dance, with origins as obscure as its name, became popular in Chicago, danced by Little Egypt at the 1893 World's Fair.

hoodlum. The most likely description of the origin of *hoodlum* is the *Oxford English Dictionary*'s "origin unknown." But there have been interesting speculations.

One of these traces the word to Bavarian dialect *hoda-lump*, with the same meaning as *hoodlum*. A more dramatic story attributes the word to *huddle 'em*, said to be used by gangs of toughs hired to beat up Chinese in San Francisco. And this is associated also with the name of one of the gang leaders, Muldoon, who was referred to as *Noodlum*. None of this is quite convincing.

hooligan. The Houlihans were a happy-go-lucky Irish family living in London in the 1890s. The *Oxford English Dictionary* identifies them as the inspiration for the word *hooligan*, now referring to a street rowdy, a ruffian, a hoodlum. Another linguist, however, identifies the word with *Hooley Gang*, the name given by Islington police to a gang led by a man named Hooley. Happy Hooligan of the 1920s comic strip had no criminal tendencies, but *hooligan* has acquired more sinister connotations in current uses.

knickers. *Knickerbocker* was a prominent Dutch name among the early settlers of New Amsterdam. Washington Irving used it as his pseudonym when writing his *History of New York*. The wide, loose trousers of these settlers, especially as shown in the illustrations for Irving's history, were called, sometimes humorously, *knickerbockers*, soon shortened to *knickers*. Knickers are generally out of fashion today, both the knee-length undergarments for women and the short, full trousers for men, buckled at the knee, formerly worn by young boys and golfers. In England, however, *knickers* has become the common term for women's panties, which seems responsible for British slang *get one's knickers in a twist,* to get flustered or agitated.

lavaliere. Louise Françoise de la Baume de La Valliere was a mistress of Louis XIV and the mother of four of his children. In 1674 she ceased to be a favorite in the court and retired to a Carmelite convent, but her early interest in jewelry is memorialized in the word *lavaliere,* for an ornament worn on a chain around the neck.

lynch. Captain William Lynch, 1742–1820, was a leader of vigilantes in Virginia. A newspaper of 1780 reports that a group of citizens were determined to stop the "iniquitous practices" of "unlawful and abandoned wretches" and "to inflict such corporal punishment on him or them as to us shall seem adequate to the crime committed." The authority for the activities of these citizens became known as Lynch law, after their leader, and the vigilante groups did generally set up courts and provide at least a semblance of legality. As the verb *lynch* developed, however, early in the nineteenth century, it came to mean to punish or execute illegally, usually to refer to a hanging carried out with no trial at all.

marcel. Marcel Grateau was a French hairdresser, and about 1875 he designed a hairstyle that became known as the marcel wave. The hairstyle lost much of its popularity at the end of the flapper era, but the word *marcel* remains.

maverick. Samuel A. Maverick, a Texas rancher, 1803–1870, failed to brand the calves in his herd, and his name was applied to any unbranded animal that might be claimed by a finder, especially a wandering motherless calf. The word *maverick* generalized to apply to a person who will not affiliate with a regular political party, and then to any independent or rebellious person.

mayonnaise. A book by Richard O'Connor, *The Irish*, comments: "Marshal MacMahon, irked by the monotony of the cuisine during an Italian campaign, commanded his chef to concoct a new sauce. It became known as mayonnaise, eventually the solace of the American housewife." The actual origin of both the dressing and its name is uncertain, but certainly MacMahon had nothing to do with it. The word was part of the English vocabulary well before MacMahon's Italian campaign, which occurred in 1859. The word existed in French early in the nineteenth century, probably identifying the sauce with Mahon, the capital of the island of Minorca.

milliner. A milliner was originally a Milaner, an inhabitant of Milan in Italy, which at one time was noted for its production of hats and other finery for women.

nicotine. Jacques Nicot was French ambassador to Lisbon, and in 1560 he bought some seeds in America for an unusual plant. He took the seeds back to France, introducing tobacco to his country, and was honored by having nicotine, the poisonous alkaloid in tobacco, named for him.

nosey parker. *Nosey* or *nosy* has long had two basic meanings, to refer to either a bad smell or an oversized nasal organ. In Australia the phrase "on the nose" still indicates that something stinks, although in America it means accurately or exactly or distinguishes a bet on a horse to place first. Both Oliver Cromwell and the Duke of Wellington had *nosey* as a nickname, celebrating their looks, not their smell or their curiosity. The use to mean inquisitive or prying turns up in print later, in the nineteenth century, especially in the phrase *nosey parker*. One possible candidate has been nominated as parent of the phrase. Matthew Parker (1504–1575) was one of England's most influential divines, and he managed to inspire bitter opposition from both Catholics and Puritans. Both sides thought of him as the instigator of investigations, but there is no real evidence that he was the original Nosey Parker.

real McCoy. An enterprising adman recently exploited etymology to promote a whiskey, confidently narrating in an advertisement "the true story" of Captain William McCoy, a smuggler in the 1920s, who supplied American speakeasies with Cutty Sark Scotch, which came to be known as "the real McCoy." The story is as plausible as some other explanations for the origin of the phrase, except that the *Oxford English Dictionary* finds the phrase in existence in the late nineteenth century, well before American Prohibition and Captain McCoy. One etymology connects the phrase to Bill McCoy, an eminent rumrunner. Another describes it as a tribute to Elijah McCoy, a Canadian inventor born in 1844, who invented in 1872 a locomotive lubricator used in trains, factories, and ships. A worker seeing a new piece of equipment would ask, "Is that the real McCoy?" Perhaps the most common explanation connects the phrase with Kid McCoy, a popular boxer who became welterweight champion in 1896. Announcements for prizefights would promise the real McCoy, not an inferior fighter. An elaboration of this attribution, sounding like folk etymology, reports that a drunk once quarreled with McCoy, refusing to believe he was a famous boxer. After he picked himself up, he said, "It's the real McCoy."

sandwich. John Montagu, the fourth earl of Sandwich, 1718–1792, became first lord of the Admiralty in England in 1740. In spite of problems in his office, including charges of bribery, the Sandwich Islands, now Hawaii, were named for him. Montagu was also known as a gambler, given to twenty-four-hour sessions at the tables, during which he refused to stop even for meals. But he did ask for slices of meat between slices of bread, to create what came to be called a *sandwich*.

scallion. Apparently there was something significant about the onions from the port of Ascolon in ancient Palestine because Latin developed the word *ascalonia* to refer to the onions of Ascalot. This was behind French *ascologne* and then English *scallion*, to refer to various kinds of spring onion. *Shallot*, for a milder onionlike vegetable, has the same origin.

shillalah. The Irish club or cudgel gets its name from the village of Shillelagh, famous for oak and blackthorn trees, whose wood produced the best shillalahs.

silhouette. Etienne de Silhouette became controller-general of France in 1759, largely through the influence of the Marquise de Pompadour, mistress of Louis XV, who had her own influence on language as the inspiration of a hairstyle still called a *pompadour*, in which the hair is piled high and straight back from the forehead with no part. Silhouette was popular at court until he proposed new taxes and other austerity measures and became identified with economy and simplification. When new forms of art—profile portraits in black and white—became popular, they were named for the controller-general, according to one guess because he was identified with simplifying and the cutouts simplified. The word *silhouette* was created in French and picked up in English.

sybarite. The ancient city of Sybaris in southern Italy became known as a center for fabulous wealth and luxury and provided the English word *sybarite* for a person devoted to luxury and pleasure, a voluptuary. *Voluptuary* comes from Latin *voluptas,* pleasure. English also acquired a word for a devotee of pleasure from the Greek, *hedonist,* from *hedone,* delight or pleasure,

tawdry. Ethelrida, a Saxon girl who died in 679, founded the cathedral at Ely and was canonized as Saint Audrey. She became patron saint of Ely, and long after her death a fair was held on her birthday. The fair gained recognition for the lace sold there, called *Saint Audrey's lace.* Commercial enterprise took over; the lace was produced in quantity and became known as cheap and gaudy. And the Saxon girl who had become a saint was forgotten as her name was slurred to *tawdry,* and *tawdry lace* was applied in the sixteenth century to a silk cord or ribbon worn as a necklace. *Tawdry lace* was shortened to just *tawdry*, describing anything showy but tasteless. One of the admirers of Macheath in John Gay's 1728 *Beggar's Opera* was called Suky Tawdry. Her name was retained in the modern adaptation of the piece, *The Threepenny Opera*, and appears in the popular song "Mack the Knife."

teetotaler. At least two stories, more or less authenticated, account for the origin of *teetotaler*. In one, the Reverend Joel Jewel, secretary of a temperance society in Hector, New York, records a meeting of January 1827 that introduced two sorts of pledges. One pledge bound signers to abstain from only distilled spirits; the other required abstinence from all alcoholic beverages, including fermented liquors. Those eschewing only distilled spirits had the letters O.P., for *old pledge*, placed after their names. Those giving up all liquor were labeled with a T for *total abstinence* and were said to have signed a T-Total pledge. Another story traces the word from England. Richard Turner, a temperance enthusiast in Preston in Lancashire, England, made a famous speech in 1833 in which he kept repeating that nothing less than t-t-t-total abstinence would do. Turner was said to be a stutterer. It is possible that both accounts are correct and the word originated independently in the two countries. Or it is possible that the word developed simply as a reduplication for emphasis of the initial letter of *total*.

vandal. The Vandals were a Teutonic tribe that ravaged Gaul and Spain and sacked Rome in A.D. 455. Although they may have done less damage to Rome than some histories suggest, their name became associated with wanton pillage, especially of art. A vandal is one who destroys property, especially cultural objects, and *vandalism* is a symbol both of barbarism and of relatively minor crimes of property destruction.

vaudeville. Compagnons du Vau-de-Vire, companions of the Vire Valley in Normandy, became famous in the seventeenth century for their topical and satirical songs. A collection of them, *Vaux de Vire*, was published in 1670, attributed for many years to a miller and singer from the area, Olivier Basselin, but probably the work of one Jean Le Houx. Even before the publication, however, the songs from the area became popular in Paris and were being inserted in farces in the theaters. With the place of the songs' origin corrupted, the farces became *Comedies avec Vaudeville*. *Vaudeville* was adopted in America to describe a variety show, with skits, singing, and dancing.

CHAPTER 7

Lore, History, Gossip, Mistakes

ANY INTERESTING WORDS ARE CREATED from events or confusions, by people who need a word or find a new use for one or misunderstand or mishear. Coal and Candle Creek near Sydney, Australia, was originally named for one Colonel Campbell. *Gringo* comes from Mexican Spanish *gringo*, meaning gibberish, presumably what English sounded like to Mexicans. *Ain't*, although it is frequently labeled "vulgar" and banned from standard English, is one of the most frequently used words in the language. *An't* developed in the late seventeenth century as a contraction for *am I not* or *are not*. *Ain't* developed as a variation on it in the early eighteenth century and began acquiring its disparaged status. Another example is *clodhopper*, a combination like *grasshopper* or *bogtrotter*, which first named a plowman, who had to hop over clods, and then came to refer to a boor or an awkward person.

applejack. *Applejack* is a liquor distilled from cider, apple brandy. In the sixteenth century *applejohn* was the name of a kind of apple considered best when it was shriveled and withered, as it was about the time of Saint John's Day in June. Shakespeare's *I Henry IV* contains the line: "I am withered like an old apple-john." Apparently, there was a notion that cider also achieved the proper maturity for distilling at about Saint John's Day, and the liquor like the apple was *applejohn*, more informally in America *applejack*.

backlog. As early as 1684 in America the log placed at the back of a fireplace was the backlog; the smaller log in front was the forestick. In the early nineteenth century, as huge log fires in cabin fireplaces disappeared, the original meaning of *backlog* lost its usefulness, and generalized figurative uses replaced it. A *backlog* became any kind of accumulation, a reserve of orders or material or jobs. Now a secretary may work at night because of a backlog of dictation or a factory may double production because of a backlog of unfilled orders. The word has also become a verb. To *backlog* an order is to put it on hold or, to use a similar metaphor, on the back burner.

bedlam. The priory of Saint Mary of Bethlehem in London was turned into a hospital for the insane in 1402. Treatment for the insane was not notably humane in early England, and the cries from Bethlehem hospital—*Bethlehem* came to be pronounced *bedlam*—inspired the use of the noun to describe noise and confusion.

blackmail. The word *blackmail* has nothing to do with the kind of mail handled by the postal service. *Mail* comes from Old English *mael* for a meeting or discussion and came in Scotland to mean rent or tribute. Early freebooting Scottish chiefs exacted tribute from small farmers in return for protecting them from being plundered. If they paid the rent or tribute, the mail, in cattle, it was called blackmail; if they paid in silver it was whitemail. *Mail,* for what is delivered by a postman, comes from Old French *male,* a wallet or bag, and originally referred to the leather pouch in which letters were carried. A still different *mail* refers to a kind of armor worn by knights of old, as in *chain mail.* This word comes through French from Latin *macula,* spot or mesh; *mesh* described the armor.

blindfold. Although a cloth may be folded to cover someone's eyes, the word *blindfold* has nothing to do with folding. The word was formed from Anglo-Saxon *fellen*, meaning to fall or strike. Middle English *blindfellen* meant to strike blind, and *blindfelled* was altered to *blindfold*. The origin of the name of *blindman's buff* adds to the notion of striking or hitting. The *buff* comes from the word *buffet*, meaning to hit or knock about. The American variation on the name of the game, *blindman's bluff*, probably developed as a mispronunciation and a kind of folk etymology, thinking that the game somehow involves the players in bluffing. A quite different word *buff* came from *buffe*, meaning buffalo, and *buff* was a yellow-brownish leather made from the skin of a buffalo or ox. The leather was sometimes used to cover a stick used for cleaning or polishing, and from this use the language acquired the verb *to buff*, meaning to polish. The color of the leather was the basis for other meanings of *buff*, and early in the twentieth century volunteer firefighters in New York City wore buff-colored, yellow-brown, uniforms. The uniforms provided a name for enthusiasts for watching fires, and then the term generalized to apply to any kind of enthusiast: "an art buff" or "a Civil War buff." Also, apparently from the color, as early as the seventeenth century, *buff* or *in the buff* came to mean naked.

boondoggle. Anyone who ever attended Boy Scout camp will remember plaiting a cord out of strips of leather —and not finding much use for it. About 1935 a scoutmaster named R. H. Link is supposed to have coined the name *boondoggle* for these braided cords and for the activity producing them. One speculation is that he coined the word by combining the last name of Daniel Boone and *joggle,* a guess for which I find no evidence. It was easy to apply the word to some of the make-work tasks in government projects during the days of recovery from the Depression, jobs that were considered pointless or unnecessary, and then to any useless or wasteful work.

bootleg. During the Prohibition period in the early twentieth century in America, some sellers of illegal liquor hid bottles in their high boots. Methods of smuggling alcoholic beverages became much more sophisticated, but the more primitive practice gave its name to the enterprise. The word stuck and gained extended meanings, so that anything, such as a recording or a book, made without authorization can be called bootleg. Even a play in football in which the quarterback carries the ball deceptively is known as a bootleg play.

chauffeur. Latin *califacere,* to make warm, is the origin of French *chauffer,* a stoker or fireman. When the automobile was introduced early in the twentieth century, the French, partly humorously, applied the word *chauffeur*, or stoker, to a professional driver, especially pertinent to early steam-driven cars. English adopted the word, but also adopted Old French *chaufer*, to warm, as *chafe*, to rub so as to stimulate or make warm. Now the notion of warming has generally disappeared, and *to chafe* is to irritate by rubbing or, by extension, to become angry or irritable, as in "chafe at the bit." *Chafing dish* preserves the earlier sense of heat.

cocktail. Nobody really knows where *cocktail* came from, but some fifty or sixty proposed etymologies have been recorded. Perhaps the most frequently cited story connects the word with French *coquetier*, an egg cup. A New Orleans bartender, Antoine Peychaud, about 1800 supposedly invented a drink using brandy made by Sazerac du Forge et Fils and served it in an egg cup, calling it a sazerac cocktail. A similar suggestion is that the word came from French *coquetel*, a mixed drink known for centuries in the vicinity of Bordeaux. It was supposedly introduced to America by French officers during the Revolution. An ingenious suggestion derives the word as a combination of *cock*, an old word for a spigot, and *tailings*, dregs or leavings. When the liquor barrels were nearly empty, the dregs from various barrels, the *cocktailings*, were thrown together, and the mixture, perhaps sold at a discount, was a cocktail. Several proposals derive the word from cockfighting—for example, from a mixture of spirits and bitters and various other ingredients called *cock-ale* and fed to cocks to prepare them for a match. *Cocktail* appeared in print in America as early as 1806, when a writer used it to name a drink that he said was "of great use to a democratic candidate, because a person having swallowed a glass of it, is ready to swallow anything else."

distaff. The development of *distaff* as a symbol for women or women's concerns indicates attitudes about the proper place for women in society. The word is a combination of Old English *dis*, flax, and *stæf*, a staff, and was the name for the staff around which flax or wool was wound in spinning. A woman was supposed to spend her time around the spinning wheel.

eavesdropper. The *eavesdrop* is the water dripping from the eaves of a house and also the area next to the building where such water falls. Someone standing in the eavesdrop to listen at a window came to be called an eavesdropper, and the term generalized to refer to anyone secretly listening to a conversation.

eighty-six. As a verb *eighty-six* has wide use in restaurants and bars; to *eighty-six* is to throw somebody out, usually with a warning against returning. As a noun the word can refer to a person not to be served, to a glass of water served but not followed by an order, or to a menu item that is no longer available. The term is primarily American, but the most common explanation for its origin is that it is British rhyming slang, to rhyme with *nix*. Why the term should be *eighty-six* rather than *sixty-six* or *thirty-six* is unclear, and some other proposed origins seem equally plausible. One story is that in the American West, where the term still seems most common, the standard bar drink was 100-proof whiskey. Later a milder whiskey, 86-proof, was introduced, supposedly for ladies. If a customer drank too much of the 100-proof, he was given the ladies' drink; that is, he was *eighty-sixed*.

fettle. Anglo-Saxon *fetel* was a belt; and since a belt is used to gird up something, *fettle* came to mean prepare or make ready, and as a noun to refer to state of preparation or condition. The word survives only in set phrases with adjectives like *fine* or *splendid*. Interestingly the word seems appropriate only for favorable states. Nobody is ever said to be in bad fettle.

flummery. Welsh *llmyru* named a food made from oatmeal or wheatmeal, and the word was adapted in English as *flummery,* also a food, especially a thick boiled oatmeal or flour. It is perhaps an indication of the quality of the food that by the early eighteenth century *flummery* had come to mean nonsense or empty talk. A possibly un-fair parallel is *hogwash,* the slop fed to pigs, which very early acquired a secondary meaning like that of *flummery.* In nineteenth-century America our penchant for fancy diction took us a step further, and we created *flummerdid-dle,* which referred to a food but usually meant to cheat and had a variety of improper meanings. In 1857 *Harper's Magazine* printed a recipe for flummerdiddle: "stale bread, pork fat, molasses, water, cinnamon, allspice, and cloves. It is a kind of mush baked in the oven."

goody. *Good,* from Anglo-Saxon *god,* became in mod-ern English a general term of approval or commendation and developed many uses. *Goodwife* appeared in the six-teenth century as an early equivalent of *Mrs.,* the mistress of a household. When *goodwife* was abbreviated to *goody,* however, it was a term of address applied to a woman in humble life. Both Samuel Johnson and Thomas Sheridan in their eighteenth-century dictionaries define the word only as "a low term of civility used to mean persons." In the eighteenth century *goody* acquired other meanings, to refer to something attractive, especially to eat, and to work as an expression of delight or surprise, often as "goody, goody." Goody Two-Shoes was a character in an eigh-teenth-century children's story, and she was popular enough to make "goody two-shoes" a label for a prissy or cloyingly nice person. Usually, however, *goody* was only a title or form of address. The degeneration of *goody* from *goodwife* is like the development of *hussy* from the quite respectable *housewife*.

gossamer. In Middle English *gossamer* was literally goose summer, a warm period in the fall, when geese were plucked and eaten. It was also a time when filmy cobwebs were likely to be floating around, looking like goose down. *Gossamer* became attached to the webs and tufts in the air and then was extended to refer to a thin, gauzelike fabric.

hobby. *Hob,* from *Rob* or *Robert,* was a name for a country fellow or rustic and sometimes a name for Puck or Robin Goodfellow or any elf or goblin. *Hobby,* a diminutive of *hob,* was used to refer to a horse, especially a plow horse. In the medieval morris dance a hobbyhorse was the figure of a horse attached to the waist of a performer, who seemed to be riding. A hobbyhorse is also a child's toy, a stick with a horse's head attached. Riding a hobbyhorse was not serious business, and a *hobby* is a pastime or spare-time activity. Riding a hobbyhorse is showing excessive interest in a favorite topic.

hobo. The *Oxford English Dictionary* on *hobo* says "origin unknown," obviously the safest conclusion. But the word has attracted speculation, some by scholars. A few dictionaries, for example, suggest that migrant workers called "ho beau" or "hello beau" as a greeting and provided an origin for the word. A popular notion is that both railroad workers and farmhands during Gold Rush days were called "hoe boys" from the implements they used. One scholar discovered a Japanese word with a plural form *hobo*, meaning everywhere. Without much evidence others have tried derivations from *oboe*, *homeward bound*, *Hoboken*, and *homus bonum*, a good fellow.

hollow. Anglo-Saxon *hohl* is the ancestor of *holwe*, which became *hollow*, and also of *hol*, which became *hole*. Curiously, the adjective *hollow* developed two almost opposite figurative meanings. In its most common figurative use the word means empty or false, as in "hollow hearts" or "a hollow mockery" or "a hollow victory." But in the seventeenth century it also could be used to mean thorough or complete, especially in the expression *all hollow*. Washington Irving comments that "Daredevil beat the goblin horse all hollow." The word can also be used adverbially in this sense without *all*: "Squire Burton won the match hollow."

hussy. Early English *huse*, house, and *wif*, wife, combined to make Middle English *huswife*, a wife who kept house and was quite respectable. By the sixteenth century it had been shortened to *hussy*, and a century later its connotations had shifted so that a hussy was not respectable, often a bawd. Johnson's eighteenth-century dictionary defines the word: "A sorry or bad woman, a worthless wench." *Goodwife* was similarly abbreviated, and *goody* was formerly used as a term of address.

jazz. The obscure origin of *jazz* has inspired a good deal of etymological speculation. There have been, for example, attempts to relate the word to various early black musicians—a dancing slave called Jass or Jazz or a Chicago musician named Jasbo Brown. One etymologist relates the word to a Louisiana-French verb *jaser,* to speed up. Another derives *jazz* from a Creole patois word *jass,* a sexual term applied to Congo dances. But as H. L. Mencken put it, "the plain fact is that *to jazz* has long had the meaning in American folk-speech of to engage in sexual intercourse, and is so defined by many lexicographers." Applications of the noun form of the word to music may have occurred as early as 1890; Jelly Roll Morton started using the word in 1902. The first New York *jazz band* appeared in 1917. The verb kept its early taboo sense, although it is less common than it once was, and the use of the noun in music has produced a number of variations. *To jazz up* is to speed up or enliven or make more exciting. The noun *jazz* has generalized to refer to anything vaguely related to a topic: "She likes books and art and all that jazz."

jerkwater. In nineteenth-century America, trains in remote areas sometimes had to stop and form a bucket brigade to jerk water from a creek to fill the tank in the tender. The Santa Fe was called the Jerkwater Line. The term generalized to suggest anything insignificant or small, but particularly a jerkwater town, so unimportant that a train would stop there only to get water.

murmur. Murmur goes back to Latin *murmur*, but apparently originated by onomatopoeia, as an echoic word like *hiss, fizz, sizzle*. Tennyson exploits the parallel in sound and meaning in

> The moan of doves in immemorial elms,
> And murmuring of innumerable bees.

pep. *Pep* appeared as American slang in the early twentieth century as an abbreviation of *pepper*. It meant something like energy or spirit or animation, and a person might be described as "full of pep." Its success as a fad word waned, but it is now standard in a number of phrases: *pep rally, pep talk, pep pill*.

sawbuck. A *sawbuck* or *sawhorse*, a frame for holding a log to be cut, was made with two supports crossed at each end so that the log could rest between them on top. The crossed end supports formed an X. X is ten in Roman numerals, which explains why a ten-dollar or ten-buck bill is a sawbuck. Deerskin or buckskin was a common trade currency in frontier America. *Buckskin* was shortened to *buck* and later transferred to the new exchange unit, a dollar bill.

seedy. *Seed* goes back to the Indo-European base **sei,* to cast or throw, and has had its current basic meaning since Old English times, developed because seeds are sowed or thrown. *Seedy* apparently developed because plants when they mature and "go to seed" often wither and die. In one common use *seedy* means in poor health or low spirits. Francis Grose's eighteenth-century slang dictionary defines *seedy* as "poor, penniless, stiver-cramped, exhausted." (A stiver was a small, almost worthless Dutch coin, and anyone stiver-cramped needed money.) Today the most common meaning is shabby or run-down or squalid. *Seed* in sports represents a different extension, referring to the practice of distributing or *seeding* the most skillful participants throughout a tournament, so that the closest contests occur in the final rounds. To seed a mine is to plant samples of rich ore so that anyone inspecting the mine gets an exaggerated impression of its value.

shebang. An Anglo-Irish word *shebeen* was in use in

the eighteenth century as a name for an unlicensed pub. In South Africa a woman running such an illegal establishment was a shebeen queen. Apparently as an adaptation of *shebeen* the word *shebang* developed in the United States as slang for a poor, usually temporary, living place, during the Civil War a soldier's tent, and also for a disreputable drinking establishment, a shebeen. It generalized to refer broadly to a series of actions, a collection of possessions, everything, in "the whole shebang."

shitepoke. Various kinds of small herons—blue, green, and night—are referred to as *shitepokes*. The name apparently originated because of an alleged tendency of the bird to defecate when disturbed. One explanation, not confirmed by ornithologists, is that the bird has an anatomical peculiarity, a straight alimentary canal, unimpeded from gullet to exit. The name is most used, however, as a term of opprobrium, to call somebody a lout or a rascal, without much awareness of the bird. And this use for the word may have developed independently, long before the heron was saddled with it. Captain Francis Grose's *Dictionary of the Vulgar Tongue* lists *sh-t sack* as "a dastardly fellow; a non-conformist." The word also appears as *shagpoke,* which may be an attempt to avoid echoes of the word's vulgar origins.

simplistic. *Simple* comes through Old French from

Latin *simplex,* meaning simple, literally having only one part. It developed a variety of meanings, one of them to designate a drug or medicine formed with a single ingredient. Thomas Browne writes: "From the knowledge of Simples, she had a Receipt to make white hair black." *Simplistic* was formed as an adjective from this use and meant pertaining to simples, drugs. About the middle of the nineteenth century, however, *simplistic* developed its current sense, to mean oversimple, ignoring complexities. *Simplified* is usually a favorable description; *simplistic* is usually unfavorable.

sixes and sevens. Chaucer's Pandarus urges Troilus to "manly set the world on six and seven," even if he thereby dies a martyr. Two centuries later Nicholas Udall cites "to settle all on six & seven" as a proverb meaning to risk everything. In Shakespeare's *Richard II,* York describes the state of the nation: "All is uneven, and everything is left at six and seven." The phrase has been around a long time, and there seems to be general agreement that it derives from dicing, referring to a risky bet; but nobody is sure why. One unsatisfactory guess is that the phrase comes from French numbers for five and six, the highest numbers on a die, but it's hard to see how five became seven. Another guess is that since there is no seven on a die, the phrase suggests a hopeless bet. Probably in some game no longer known six and seven were considered hard points to make.

slapstick. The name for humor featuring banana peels and prat falls and flying custard pies comes from a device used in early comedy, perhaps as early as seventeenth-century pantomimes. Two boards were fastened at one end and designed as a percussion instrument, especially useful to emphasize the sound of a blow administered by a clown to the rear of another character.

slogan. *Slogan*, now mainly a catchphrase identifying a political campaign or advertising a product, began as a war cry used by Scottish and Irish clans. The Gaelic words *sluggh*, army, and *ghairm*, yell, combined as *slugghghairm*, meaning a battle cry.

son of a gun. One of the most widespread fanciful etymologies is a story explaining the origin of *son of a gun*. According to the account, the expression sprang from the love life of sailors on British warships, who were sometimes visited on board by wives. Convenient privacy on the ship was available under the gun turrets, which became marital as well as martial beds. An offspring of this cannon-covered union was a son of a gun. A slang dictionary of 1889 is even more specific and more positive. It quotes: "One admiral declared he was literally thus cradled, under the breast of a gun carriage." The idea had earlier expression in Jon Bee's dictionary of 1823, which defines *son of a gun* as "a soldier's bastard." But the expression was in the language as a term of disrespect at least a century earlier than any of these explanations. It seems almost certainly to have been created as a euphemism for *son of a bitch,* like *dang* for *damn* or *gosh* or *golly* for *God. Son of a bitch* is one of the most common of insults and has parallels in many languages. It was highly offensive in English for centuries, generally interpreted literally. Kent in Shakespeare's *King Lear* calls Oswald "the son and heir of a mongrel bitch." By the time of World War I, *son of a bitch* was used with almost no consciousness of its literal meaning, and it became so much a part of the language of American soldiers that for a generation after the war Americans in France were known as *les sommombiches.*

spider. The eight-legged arachnid gets its name from its most obvious activity, from Anglo-Saxon *spinnen.* When cooking was often done on an open fire, frying pans were made on legs to stand above the coals. The utensil looked like a spider, and in some American dialects, especially in New England, a skillet is called a spider.

stump. Middle English *stumpe* referred to what was left of a tree after part of it had been cut off. It came to refer specifically to the projecting portion of the trunk of a felled or fallen tree that remains fixed in the ground. Generally the word extended to apply to all sorts of things that were somehow like the stump of a tree—the part remaining when a leg has been amputated, a pencil or candle that has been shortened from its original length, the part of a broken tooth left in the gums, a docked tail on an animal. Especially in early American political campaigns, a candidate often found a tree stump the best platform, and "to make a stump speech" or "take to the stump" developed. "To be up a stump" is like being up the creek, stuck in some kind of difficult spot. "To stir one's stumps" depends on the parallel between the base of a tree and the base of a person. In cricket, stumps are sticks that are parts of wickets, and one way to put a batter out is to stump him by knocking over a stump at the right moment. This use may have influenced the development of the American verb *to stump*, meaning to confuse or baffle.

tack. *Tack* was *takke* in Middle English and goes back to French *tache*, a nail, and Germanic *tacke*, a point. It still refers primarily to a small nail; for some reason *brass tacks* in America and sometimes *tin tacks* in England are the ones to get down to. Extensions of the word's meaning are interesting. The word generalized to refer to various kinds of fastenings, and in nautical use it named a rope used to fasten a sail to a boom. Using the tack changed the course of a ship, adjusting to different directions of the wind. And this generalized to refer to any course of action; a political campaign can be on the wrong tack or can try a new one. It's unclear how the word came to refer to food as in *hardtack* or to equipment for harnessing a horse.

tinker's dam or **damn**. Tinkers, menders of pots and pans, were often tramps who moved from town to town looking for household jobs. Christopher Sly in Shakespeare's *Taming of the Shrew* was a drunken tinker, and an Elizabethan statute provided for sentencing "all jugglers, tinkers and petty chapmen" and other vagrants who were "rogues, vagabonds, and sturdy beggars." Francis Grose's 1785 *Dictionary of the Vulgar Tongue* points out that a *dam* was a small Indian coin and suggests that "I don't care a dam," like "I don't care half a farthing," reflects the uselessness of the coin. But the phrase "don't care a curse" or "not worth a curse" was also in the language by the fifteenth century, and *damn* got into such phrases as a specific curse. The *Oxford English Dictionary* has an entry for *tinker's damn*, but not *tinker's dam*. The case for *dam* is supported by the fact that tinkers in the nineteenth century used what they called a dam in their repair work. To repair a hole in a kettle, the tinker built a mold of sand or sometimes bread around the hole, a dam, and poured in molten metal. The dam was discarded after the repair. Today something worthless can be not worth a tinker's damn or a tinker's dam, depending on whether one prefers a tinker's unreliable oath or his worthless coin or discarded mold. Nobody ever says that something *is* worth a tinker's damn or dam.

tommyrot. *Tommy,* of course, is the common nickname for *Thomas,* and in some parts of England at least, *tommy* refers to bread distributed to the poor on Saint Thomas's Day, December 21. Probably from this use the word came to refer to brown bread provided for soldiers and still more generally to food taken to work or school for lunch. Buttercup in *HMS Pinafore* includes among her wares "soft tommy and succulent chops." But *Tom* or *tom* is also a name used to designate a man or boy whose name is unknown—like *Jack* or *Mac* or *Tom, Dick, and Harry*—and we have *tom turkey, tomcat, tomfool,* and *Tom o'Bedlam. Tommy* in the sense of food is probably behind *tommyrot,* nonsense or rubbish, and the quality of the bread in military rations is probably involved. *Tommy Adkins* or just *Tommy* to refer to a British soldier comes from the use in the early nineteenth century of *Thomas Adkins* as a specimen signature on military forms. *Tommy gun* is an abbreviation for a Thompson machine gun.

willies. Always used with *the*, *willies* developed in America in the late nineteenth century to mean nervousness or apprehension: "to have the willies." The origin is unknown, but the best guess is that it comes from *willy-nilly*, which appeared in English in the early seventeenth century. The word is a shortening of *will I, nill I*, meaning "do I wish or not wish." It is used to mean whether one likes or not, as in "They had to conform willy-nilly." Or it may mean haphazardly or at random, as in "The cars were parked willy-nilly in the lot." Similarly *shilly-shally* developed from repetition of *shall*, to mean vacillate or act hesitantly, "shall I, shall I not." *Dilly-dally* and *wishy-washy* have a similar pattern, and in England *hitty-missy* appeared in the sixteenth century, although it is now rare.

wool-gathering. The phrase turns up as early as the end of the sixteenth century and apparently refers to the custom in an earlier and more thrifty society of gathering the fugitive tufts of wool left by sheep on bushes and hedges. Sheep roam, and the bits of wool were scattered over a wide area. The gathering involved much wandering, often to little purpose; thus *wool-gathering* was readily applied to any indulgence in idle fancy or daydreaming or to any foolish or fruitless pursuit.

yokel. One speculation derives *yokel* from *yokel* or *youkell*, which were dialect forms of *hickwall*, a green woodpecker. Compare the use of *peckerwood*, an inversion of *woodpecker*, in nineteenth-century America to refer to a poor white in the South. Another theory relates *yokel* to *yoke*, the frame used to join two oxen so that they could pull together. The yokel was an ox driver. The most common dictionary etymology for the word is "origin obscure."

CHAPTER 8

Compounding and Affixes

P ERHAPS THE MOST COMMON METHOD OF word formation today is combining existing elements—word roots or common affixes—to create new meanings. Some self-explaining compounds were formed long ago, but many are more recent to meet new needs. *Hardware* has been in the language for centuries, but *software*, *database*, *jetport*, and *heliport* are more recent. We have also created many words by combining elements derived from Latin or Greek. Greek *autos*, self, and Latin *mobilis*, movable, were put together to make *auto-*

mobile, when we needed a name for a new, self-moving vehicle. The French combined Greek *helix,* a spiral, and *pterion,* wing, to produce *hélicoptère,* and English adopted it. Greek *orthos,* straight, and *odont,* tooth, were combined to make *orthodontist,* a dentist who straightens teeth; *orthos* plus *doxa,* opinion, produced *orthodox.* Common prefixes have continued to be useful in word formation—from Latin *ab-,* from; *ante-,* before; *cum-,* with; from Greek *anti-,* against; *auto-,* self; *neo-,* new. *Pre-,* before; *trans-,* across; and *post-,* after, have produced *prehistoric, transoceanic, postgraduate.* Popular creations with suffixes include *stardom, pollster, racketeer,* and advertising favorites with suffixes like *-ery, -orium, -orama, -burger: eatery, lubritorium, seafoodorama, fishburger.*

accolade. *Accolade* was formed by combining the Latin prefix *ad-,* to, with *collum,* neck. It specified an embrace used in conferring knighthood, later a tap on the shoulder with the flat of a sword. It has generalized to refer to any recognition of merit, words of approval, an award.

adroit. Probably because most human beings are right-handed, language has tended to create words with favorable connotations associated with the right hand. French *a-,* to or toward, plus *droit,* right, produced English *adroit,* clever and skillful. English, however, has adopted French *gauche*, left, to mean awkward, lacking social grace. *Gawky* is related to dialect *gawk*, left-handed. Latin *dexter*, right or to the right, is the origin of English *dexterous*, skillful. English adopted the Latin word for left, *sinister*, retaining its original meaning in expressions like *bar sinister* in a coat of arms but also meaning threatening or ominous.

adult. Both *adult* and *adolescent* go back to Latin *alere*, to feed or sustain, which acquired the prefix *ad-*, to, and became *adalescere*, to increase or to grow. The English words specialized to indicate different stages of maturing. *Adult*, from attempts to distinguish what is appropriate for grownups but not children, has acquired a new meaning, risqué or obscene, as in "adult movies" or "adult language." *Adultery* is not, as might be suspected, the state of being an adult, but a quite different word. It comes from Latin *adulterare*, to falsify, which also is the origin of English *adulterate*, to make inferior by adding a poor or improper substance.

antimacassar. The Greek prefix *anti-*, against, opposite, is readily used to create new compounds with self-evident meanings: *antifreeze, anti-inflation, antiaircraft*. It also combined with Greek roots to create a number of words. *Anti-* plus Greek *tithenai*, to place, is *antithesis*, a contrast or opposition of thoughts. The prefix plus *pathein,* to suffer or feel, produced *antipathy. Antiseptic* derives from *anti-* plus Greek *sepein,* to make putrid. *Antagonize* derives from *anti-* plus Greek *agonizesthai,* to contend or struggle. *Anti-* also is part of *antimacassar.* Macassar is a port in Celebes in the Netherlands Indies, and *macassar oil* was the commercial name given to a hair dressing that was heralded as a combination of exotic ingredients shipped from Macassar, although it was apparently mainly coconut oil. An 1895 advertisement heralds Rowland's Macassar Oil as "the best and safest preserver of the hair. . . . It nourishes, preserves, and strengthens the hair, prevents baldness, and is the best brilliantine." The oil and other hair dressings like it were also effective in staining the backs of chairs, and the doilies or covers used to prevent this sort of soiling were called *antimacassars.*

auger. *Auger,* the name of a tool for boring holes in wood or in the earth, developed from Anglo-Saxon compounding. *Nafu,* the nave or hub of a wheel, and *gar,* a spear, combined to make *nafogar,* a drill used on wheels. This became *nauger* in Middle English, and then by the same kind of faulty division that produced *adder* and *apron, a nauger* became *an auger.*

bailiwick. A bailiff in early England had jurisdiction over a village or part of an estate. Combining *bailiff* with *wike,* Anglo-Saxon for village, produced *bailiwick,* the area under a bailiff's jurisdiction, and by extension one's special field of interest or authority.

bankrupt. Early money changers conducted their business sitting on a bench, *banque* in French and *banca* in Italian, and then *bank* in English for a more complex institution. When a money changer's business failed, it was said that his bench was broken, and both French and Italian developed words derived by combining their word for bench with Latin *rumpere,* to break, *banqueroute* and *banca rotta.* These produced English *bankrupt,* which has extended in meaning to refer loosely to any inadequacy, as in "mental bankrupt."

cataclysm. The Greek prefix *kata-,* down, plus *klyzein,* to wash, produced the word for a great flood or deluge, which has generalized to any kind of disaster, earthquake, or war. The word is one of many formed in English with the prefix *kata-,* which can mean against or wholly as well as down. *Catechism* comes from *kata-* and *echeo,* sound; the question and answer procedure was once handed down orally, as sound. *Catacombs,* for underground burial vaults, came from *kata-,* down, and *kymbe,* hollow. *Kata-* and *sedra,* seat, produced *cathedra,* the throne of a bishop, and *cathedral,* the main church of a bishop's see, housing the cathedra. *Catarrh,* an inflammation causing an increased flow of mucus, came from *kata-* and *rhein,* to flow.

companion. Latin *cum,* with, and *panis,* bread, are the origin of English *companion,* literally one who eats bread with you. A *company* was originally a group of people who shared hospitality. *Company* has generalized in various ways, and a business company or a military unit is no longer associated with bread-breaking.

daisy. Anglo-Saxon *dæges* and *eage* were combined to mean day's eye, to provide a name for the flower with bright petals and a sunburst center being revealed in the morning.

dandelion. The flower got its name from its pointed, toothlike leaves from French *dent de lion,* tooth of the lion.

delirium. A person who is "off his rocker" might be considered delirious. The rocker in the phrase is apparently the piece of wood that allows a chair or cradle to rock. *Delirium* developed with the same logic as the slang phrase. It comes from Latin *de-,* from, and *lira,* a track or furrow. A delirious person is off the track.

desultory. A desultory conversation jumps from one thing to another, is not methodical. *Desultory* comes from Latin *de-,* down, plus *salire,* to leap or jump.

dis or **diss.** The verb *dis* is interesting because it seems to be a prefix turned into a verb, created as slang in America as recently as the 1980s to refer to any kind of put-down, especially disparaging or insulting talk. And it seems to have moved into standard journalistic use, especially in political comment, where one candidate is described as dissing another. In England, slang *dis* developed somewhat earlier, apparently as an abbreviation of *disconnected*, meaning broken, not working: "The poor fellow's brain's going dis." Similar is the use of *dish* meaning to ruin, to completely defeat: "The scandal completely dished his chance for election."

disgruntled. The verb *gruntle* existed in the late sixteenth century, usually referring to a pig, and meaning to utter a little grunt. More generally it meant to grumble or complain. It became obsolete, but in the middle of the seventeenth century it was combined with the prefix *dis-*, mainly an intensive meaning something like utterly, in what was probably a partly humorous word, *disgruntle*, meaning to put into a sulky mood, to make discontented. It appears now usually in the adjective form, *disgruntled*, out of sorts, annoyed, disappointed. Curiously in the twentieth century, *gruntled* has had a usually humorous revival but with a different meaning. Apparently on the assumption that *disgruntled* is a negative, the back formation *gruntled* means pleased or satisfied or content. James

Thurber refers to journalists in Paris as "the most gruntled group I ever knew."

dishevel. Latin *capillus*, hair, is behind French *chevel*, hair, which combined with the prefix *dis-* to produce Middle English *dischevelen*, to tear out hair. The word generalized to refer to any kind of rumpling or disarrangement, of clothing as well as hair. In the early seventeenth century, the word *sheveled* developed. But it was not a positive of *disheveled*. It was formed by aphesis, a fancy term for dropping a syllable, like dropping the *es* in *esquire* to form *squire*. *Sheveled* is now archaic, but it meant *disheveled*. The association of neat hair with general tidiness is also reflected in the development of *unkempt* to mean messy or slovenly, especially as a result of neglect—"an unkempt lawn" or "an unkempt ragamuffin." *Kempt* derives from Anglo-Saxon *camb*, a comb, and in early English *unkempt* meant uncombed. *Kempt* is not much used today, although it does appear in some dictionaries.

egregious. Latin *grex*, *gregis* named a herd and is the origin of English *gregarious*, to describe someone who likes to be with the herd, likes company, is sociable. But the Latin root was combined with various prefixes to produce other words. With Latin *con-*, with, *grex* is the root of *congregation*, which may be people herded together by a shepherd or pastor. *Se-*, away, plus *grex*, produced *segregate*, to separate from others. *Integrate*, the opposite of *segregate*, however, has a different origin, from Latin *integare*, to make whole or complete. *Egregious* comes from *e-*, out, plus *grex* and originally meant outside the herd, out of the ordinary, outstanding. But that meaning is now archaic, and the word refers to something outside the herd in a different way, something remarkable for undesirable qualities, flagrantly bad.

eliminate. The Latin word *limen* meant threshold or door; with the prefix *e-*, out, *eliminare* meant to turn out of doors. English made *eliminate* more general, to omit, reject, get rid of. Latin *limen*, with a different prefix, *pre-*, before, is also behind *preliminary*, coming before the threshold or the beginning of the main action.

entice. Old French *enticier* came from Latin *in-* plus *titio*, a firebrand, and meant to set afire. To entice is to kindle interest with promises of pleasure or reward.

exquisite. Latin *quaerere*, to search, combined with the prefix *ex-* and produced *exquirere*, to search out. The verb's participal form *exquisitus* was adopted in English, and *exquisite* originally meant carefully sought out, choice. It has kept some of that meaning in phrases like "exquisite design" or "exquisite lace," but it has also generalized as a term of praise or approval. It has alternative pronunciations, with the accent on either the first or the second syllable. A few other English words are pronounced with the accent on either the first or the second syllable: *hospitable, despicable, formidable*.

gossip. *Sib* in Old English, as today, referred to a relative, especially a brother or sister, and also produced *sibling,* which is more common. Old English also combined *God* with *sib* to produce *godsib* as the name for a sponsor at a christening, especially a godmother or godfather. The word became *gossip* and was extended to refer to good companions or friends, and then to refer to news or idle chatter.

illusion. Latin combined *in-*, on, with *ludere,* play, to produce *illudere,* to mock or jeer. English *illusion,* a false idea or a deception, came from *illusus,* a form of *illudere.*

innocuous. Latin *nocere,* to hurt or injure, produced English *noxious,* harmful to health or morals, and also *obnoxious,* with the prefix *ob-*, completely or totally, to mean very objectionable or offensive. Combined with the prefix *in-*, not, however, *nocere* is behind *innocuous,* harmless, insignificant.

lieutenant. A *lieutenant* is someone who takes the place of another, often acting for a superior. The title comes from Latin *locus,* place, through Old French *lieu,* place, combined with Latin *tenere*, to hold. The word is pronounced "leftenant" in England.

nasturtium. The Roman naturalist Pliny observed that Latin *nasus*, nose, and *tortus*, from *torquere*, to twist, were combined to indicate that the nasturtium, because of its pungent smell, was a nose twister.

nickname. *Ekename* was a Middle English compound of *eke*, other or additional, and *name*. It became *nickname* by syllabic merging. As *an ekename* was pronounced, the *n* of *an* stuck to what followed it. In the same way the word *newt* was formed by merging *an* and *eute*, the Middle English name for a small lizard. The opposite process produced *adder* from *nadder* and *apron* from *napron*.

orangutan. The Malay word for man was *oran;* combined with *utan* for forest it meant a wild man. Europeans applied the word to apes of the Dutch East Indies in the seventeenth century. The main character in Thomas Love Peacock's satirical romance *Melincourt* (1817) is Sir Oran Haut-ton, an orangutan, who has been educated by a rich young philosopher to everything except speech and has become an amiable and chivalrous gentleman who plays admirably on the flute.

paradox. The prefix *para-*, from Greek, has a variety of meanings in English: beside, beyond, aside from, past.

Meaning beyond, it combined with Greek *doxa*, opinion, to produce *paradox*, a statement beyond belief. A paradox is a contradiction, a statement that seems unbelievable or even self-contradictory, but may actually be true. Clifford Odets defines "a paradox in human behavior: he shoots you for a nickel; for fifty bucks he sends you flowers." The prefix occurs in many other words in English. It combined with Greek *phraʒein*, to tell, to produce *paraphraʒein*, to say in other words, which became modern English *paraphrase*. Greek *pherne*, a dowry, joined with *para-* to produce Latin *parapherna*, what a bride brought with her to a marriage in addition to her dowry. The dowry went to the husband, but legally the wife could keep the *parapherna*, or in English *paraphernalia*. The word generalized in meaning and now refers to any collection of articles, equipment, apparatus. A different English prefix *para-* came from Latin *parare*, to prepare, and means protecting from. Combined with *chute*, a fall, it produced *parachute*. Combined with Latin *pectus*, breast, it produced Italian *parapetto* and then English *parapet*, a wall or barrier to screen troops from fire and then by extension a wall or railing to keep people from falling off a balcony.

penthouse. Latin *appendere*, to hang, is behind English *pend;* something pending is hanging or waiting. With the prefix *ad-* it produced *append* and *appendix,* and then with suffixes *-itis,* inflammation, and *-ectomy,* a cutting, *appendicitis* and *appendectomy. Penthouse* also goes back to *appendere,* which produced Middle English *pentis,* an addition to a structure, but it acquired its modern spelling through folk etymology. The origin of *penthouse* has nothing to do with *house,* but the final syllable of *pentis* sounded enough like *house* to make the current spelling plausible.

petticoat. English borrowed French *petit,* small, using the feminine form *petite* especially to refer to clothing sizes for women. English also adopted the French word in a few legal uses, *petit jury* and *petit larceny,* and in special uses like *petits pois* for small peas and *petits fours* for small cakes. As *petty* it was used in various compounds, including *petticoat,* which originally designated a small coat worn by men under a doublet or even a coat of mail. The word came to apply to women's clothes, and the garment became longer.

polliwog. *Polliwog* comes from Middle English *polwygle* and combines *poll,* head, with *wiggle* to produce an obviously appropriate name for a tadpole. *Tadpole* has a similar origin, from Middle English *tade,* toad, and *poll,* the toad that seems all head.

posterior. Latin *post,* after or behind, is frequently

used as a prefix in English, combined often with other Latin words. To *postpone* is to place after, *post-* plus *ponere*, place or put. *Postscript*, after the regular writing of a letter, derives from *post-* and *scribere*, write. *Postmortem*, an examination made after death, comes from *post-* plus *mors*, death. *Postdiluvian*, after the deluge, combines *post-* and *diluvium*, flood, opposite to *antediluvian*. *Postgraduate* and *postdate* use the prefix with contemporary English words. Latin *posterus*, from *post*, meant following or coming after, and is the source for *posterity*, what comes after, and *posterior*, which means coming after or situated behind, and by extension refers to the rear end of an animal or a person.

prevaricate. Latin *praevaricari* combined *prae*, before, and *varicare*, to straddle, which came from *varus*, bent. The Latin word literally meant to walk crookedly, and to *prevaricate* in English is to deal crookedly with the truth.

scuttlebutt. *Scuttle* came from Old French *escoutille*, a hatchway, which was related to Spanish *escotar*, meaning to cut a hole in a garment to make it fit. It became a nautical term for a hatch on a ship and by extension for any hole. To *scuttle* a ship was to sink it by cutting a hole in its hull. By compounding, a *water butt*, or cask, on a ship, with a hole, or *scuttle*, in it for a dipper or cup was a *scut-*

tlebutt or sometimes a *scuttlecask*. In the U.S. Navy since the 1930s the drinking fountain that succeeded the dipper and cask has been called the scuttlebutt. And the kind of talk common around the drinking fountain, especially rumor and gossip, is scuttlebutt.

stark. *Stark* comes from Anglo-Saxon to mean stiff or rigid, but it has developed other meanings through compounding. It can mean barren or desolate, or standing out sharply—"a tree stark in the snow"—or entire or utter or sheer, as in "stark terror." It can also mean naked, from a confusion that developed the phrase *stark-naked*. *Stertnaked* developed in Middle English from Anglo-Salon *steort*, meaning tail or rump. In the sixteenth century the spelling was shifted to *stark-naked,* and the phrase came to mean absolutely naked, rather than just bare-bottomed as it had earlier. In the early twentieth century British slang shortened the phrase to *starko* or *starkers:* "There was no stripping. . . . The girls were starkers all the time."

tragedy. Latin *tragoidos* was a combination of *tragos,* goat, and *oidos,* singer, and it is the ancestor of modern English *tragedy.* The Latin word came to refer to a tragic actor or singer in the Roman theater, but nobody is quite sure how goats were involved in the early history of the word. One theory is that a goat was the prize given to an actor at a dramatic festival, that he was the goat singer because he won the goat. Another proposes that the name comes from the songs sung over goats that were sacrificed to Dionysus at a drama festival. The most likely explanation is that the *tragoidus* was literally a goat singer, an actor dressed in a goatskin to represent a satyr, and then an actor in a satyric drama, the form from which tragedy in a later sense was developed.

uncouth. *Uncouth*, like many English words, was formed as a negative from a positive, *couth*, that dropped out of use after the negative became current. Anglo-Saxon *cuth* was a form of the verb *cunnan*, to know, and *un-* as a prefix meant not. *Uncouth* still may mean unknown, or strange, but usually it has the extended meaning, uncultured, crude, boorish, which developed in the eighteenth century. And then *couth* had a revival as a back formation meaning cultured or refined, frequently used humorously. In the play *Born Yesterday* Billy Dawn says to Harry Brock, "You're uncouth." He replies, "I'm just as couth as you are." In a similar development, *kempt* from Anglo-Saxon *camb*, a comb, meant combed in early English. It has pretty much gone out of use, but the negative *unkempt*, originally uncombed, has stayed in use and generalized to mean untidy or messy or even unrefined or crude. A spoof on the game of making positives by back formation from negatives appeared in a number of newspaper columns a few years ago. Dropping the *anti-* in *antithesis,* the columns produced: "The Society for the Preservation of Titheses commends your ebriated and scrutable use of delible and defatigible, which are gainly, sipid, and couth. We are gruntled and consolate that you have the ertia and eptitude to choose such putably pensible titheses, which we parage." The spoof is inaccurate in at least two of its examples. Although *antithesis* comes from Greek *antitithenai,* which might suggest *tithesis,* removing *anti-* from the English word produces *thesis.* And the *in-* of *inebriated* is not a negative but an intensive. *Ebrius* was one of several Latin terms meaning drunk, and *ebriated* and *inebriated* would mean the same.

ventriloquist. A *ventriloquist,* according to the word's origin, is someone who speaks from the belly; the word comes from Latin *loquor,* to speak, and *venter,* the belly. *Ventricle,* for chambers of the heart, also comes from *venter,* after some anatomical confusion.

whiskey, whisky. Although temperance enthusiasts may not approve the notion, distilled spirits have been honored in some languages as the "water of life"—*aquavit* in Sweden, *eau de vie* for brandy in France, both derived from Latin *aqua vitae,* water of life. Russian *vodka* is just a diminutive of *voda*, water, with no reference to the water's significance. The Scotch and Irish named their whiskey in Gaelic, *uisge*, water, plus *beatha*, life, which became *usquebaugh*, then *whiskybae*, and ultimately *whiskey*.

CHAPTER 9

Semantic Change

MANY WORD STORIES IN PREVIOUS CHAPTERS have involved the kinds of meaning change described in the introduction—degradation and elevation, specialization and generalization, metaphoric extension. For example, *aggravate* (22) and *unique* (23) still provoke usage questions about their new meanings. *Literal* (27) and *virtual* (34) have shifted to meanings almost opposite those of a hundred years ago. Many other words have changed to become, in effect, additions to the vocabulary. *Great* once meant only large in size, the opposite of *small*, but it has become a term of general approval for a dinner or a football game or the weather. The word *nice* is an interesting example. The Latin word *nescius*, ignorant, was the origin of French *nice*, foolish. The word was adopted in English in the thirteenth century, keeping its French meaning but adding the notion of fastidiousness. From this English developed the meaning of precise, as in "a nice distinction," which some purists insist is the only acceptable meaning of the word. But *nice* in current English has generalized to refer to anything as agreeable or pleasant or pleasing, a nice day or dress or party. The stories in this chapter describe words that seem to me especially interesting because of the semantic changes affecting their development.

amuse. *Amuse* has shifted in meaning since it came into English in the fifteenth century from Old French *amuser*, to stare fixedly or perhaps stupidly. The English word meant to deceive or delude or puzzle. In the sixteenth century, a soldier who amused the enemy was deceiving or misleading, not entertaining. *Divert*, from Latin *dis-*, apart, plus *vertere*, turn, has developed similarly. It meant to turn aside or deflect from a purpose, but became also a synonym of *amuse*.

appear. Basically *appear* still has the meaning of its origin from Latin *ad-*, to, plus *parare*, come forth, be visible. A person can appear in court or in a play or at a party unexpectedly. But a person can also appear to be honest, in which sense the word has acquired a quite different meaning, to seem or look.

ass. Anglo-Saxon *assa,* related to Latin *asinus,* was the name for a donkey, as is the English word *ass,* which also exploited alleged characteristics of the donkey and came to refer to a stupid or silly person. Another Anglo-Saxon word, however, *ears,* produced English *arse,* meaning rump or buttocks. The two words came to be confused, partly because of the tendency of some dialects to lose the *r* sound. As a variation of *arse, ass* became a taboo word in American English and developed a number of compounds, with *horse's* or *kiss* or *hole.* I remember a Sunday school class from my childhood on the Old Testament story of Balaam and what the teacher referred to, a little self-consciously, as his donkey. The class quickly dissolved into snickers and giggles as we could see the printed text of the lesson, with the topic clearly *Balaam and His Ass.* Interestingly, *ass* has gained a kind of near respectability in recent years, partly from use by highly placed politicians who vow to "kick ass." It is now only one of a series of slang terms for the human posterior, which are in general use although sometimes considered mildly naughty—*prat, kiester, tush, buns, fanny, duff,* *butt, derriere* (mainly a cute euphemism), *bum* (especially in England).

astronomical. *Astronomical* provides an interesting example of the way in which one characteristic of a word can develop into a new meaning. *Astronomy* comes from Greek *astron*, star, and *nomus*, law or system; an *astronomer* studies the system of stars. But since the astronomer deals with very large numbers, *astronomical* has come to mean very large. We call the national debt astronomical, even though it has nothing to do with stars.

atone. In its early uses *atone* meant to agree or to be at one with, which explains its origin from *at* combined with *one*. In the seventeenth century, it developed the meaning to make amends or reparations.

black. The story of *black* is interesting because of the varied associations it has attracted over the years and the many compounds formed with it. Its derivation is clear, from Anglo-Saxon *blaec*, going back to Indo-European **blegh*, meaning to shine or burn. Apparently the word came to designate a color associated with burning or soot. And most of the uses of *black* are to designate the opposite of *white*, the color—or colorlessness—formed by complete absorption of light. Many uses of the word simply designate appearance with no favorable or unfavorable connotations: *blackbird, blackboard, black ice, black* *and blue*. But by late Middle English the word had developed various figurative senses, meaning evil, malignant, melancholy, ominous, sinister, illegal, and so on. And about the same time the word came to be used as a designation for dark-skinned people, often used disparagingly or insultingly. In America, during the 1970s, after centuries of use as a term of disrespect to label a race, *black* became politically correct, replacing *Negro* or the earlier *colored*. *Black* remains generally acceptable, although some American leaders prefer *African American* or *Afro-American*. The result of these variations in usage is a tendency for the different meanings to get confused, for unintended implications to develop. For example, *black ball* refers to the color of a ball used in a ballot box to record an adverse vote, but the ball also acquires something of the unfavorable connotations of blackness. In *black humor* the word suggests darkness and unpleasantness, but it also has been associated with black people. The question of political correctness or whether various terms are racial slurs can be complicated, and many expressions that sometimes inspire objections seem to be completely innocent. For instance, *black sheep*, for what every family is supposed to have one of, developed in the eighteenth century and may have started with the nursery rhyme, "Baa, baa black sheep." But it certainly is intended to refer only to the odd sheep among all the white sheep and has nothing to do with race. *Black book* originated as a term for no more ominous reason than that early official books were usually bound in black. In early British universities black books were used to record cases of student misconduct. The term came to refer to any book containing a list of names, especially of persons to be given some kind of special treatment—for example, no further credit. On the other hand, some expressions—*bootblack* and *blackguard*—that originated innocently have acquired racial connotations.

bless. *Bless* and *blessing* have moved a long way from their origin in the sacrifices of early religions. The words come from Anglo-Saxon *bledsian*, the rite of consecration by sprinkling the altar with blood. *Bledsian* comes from *blod*, blood.

bloody. There is no mystery about the word *bloody* in its literal sense; it is simply a development from Anglo-Saxon *blod*. But late in the eighteenth century, in England and especially in Australia, it became an expletive, blasphemous or indecent or both, and nobody knows why. Although it is quite innocuous in the United States, it is still likely to be printed b—dy in England and to raise an eyebrow in many social circles. It seems most likely that it has religious origins, relating to Christ's blood on the cross, and akin to oaths like *s'blood* and perhaps *by'r Lady*. But the word seems to have acquired also associations with menstruation. It therefore relates to another large group of taboo words, those involving sex and the human body. A different sort of theory suggests that the word acquired its unsavory connotations from association with young *bloods* who performed various acts of vandalism during the reign of Queen Anne. There is no real evidence for any of these theories. Social attitudes toward *bloody* have relaxed, although in England the word is still associated with the "lower classes."

blue. Names for colors are among the most interesting words in the language because of the variety of meanings and associations they develop. The origin of the word *blue* is straightforward, from Old French *bleu* and Old High German *blao*, and there is no dispute about the color it designates, although there are several shades designated by adjectives: *sky, navy, midnight, powder*, or *Alice* (named for Theodore Roosevelt's daughter). John Ruskin confidently declared, "Blue color is everlastingly appointed by the Deity to be a source of delight," but the four humors of medieval physiology included black or blue bile that produced melancholy, and blue is not always a source of delight. *Blue Monday* and *blue funk* illustrate the common meaning of *blue* as depressed or unhappy. *Blue devils* developed in the eighteenth century as a term for delirium tremens or generally low spirits. It was abbreviated to *blues* and came to designate depression and also a type of music characterized by minor harmony and melancholy words. A *blue note* is flatted. One manifestation of the color produced *blue nose*, which started as a designation for a Nova Scotian, a reference to the color of a nose in a severe climate or to the blue-nose potato grown in Nova Scotia. For no obvious reason *blue nose* generalized, especially in America, to describe an excessively straitlaced or prying person, and *blue law* refers to any strict puritanical regulation. This use seems related to the association of *blue* with obscenity or lewdness as in a *blue movie* or a *blue joke,* a meaning that may go back to the fact that blue was associated with the dress of harlots. Songwriters make romantic allusions to a *blue moon,* but the phrase *once in a blue moon* depends on the fact that the moon is not blue, that a blue moon will not occur. *Blue-collar* worker suggests a preference for blue work shirts but may also echo a tradition, recorded by Pliny, that the Gauls dressed their slaves in blue.

boudoir. French *bouder*, to pout or sulk, combined with *-oir* to name what was in the Middle Ages a room where a lady could be sent to get over the sulks. Her pouting room became more generally a room for retiring or receiving close acquaintances.

brand. Anglo-Saxon *brand* or *brond* named a flame or torch, and in English a *brand* is a stick that is burning or partially burned, a *firebrand*. But the word has developed a variety of extended and figurative meanings. A firebrand, for example, is a person who incites others to action. A brand is an identifying mark burned on cattle or at one time on alleged criminals. This use generalized so that a brand is a kind or make of something, as a brand of coffee. *Brand-new* originally meant fresh from the fire, applied to metal objects just forged, then to anything new.

bug. Nobody is quite sure of the origin of *bug*, as a nonscientific name for a variety of insects. The Welsh word *bwg*, for a ghost or hobgoblin, apparently is behind an English word *bug*, for an imaginary object of terror, a bugbear or bogey. This *bug* became obsolete in the nineteenth century, but on the theory that some insects are frightening it may be responsible for the current *bug*, which has developed a variety of new meanings. A bug may be a concealed microphone, or it may be a fault or malfunction in a machine or a computer. *To bug* somebody may mean to place a listening device in a telephone or simply to be a steady annoyance. In one's ear a bug may be a forewarning or an idea or a bit of gossip. *Bug juice* is cheap whiskey, from the tobacco-colored secretion of a grasshopper. A person with some kind of enthusiasm or obsession may be a bug—an antique car bug or a soccer bug. *Bug out* or *off* complicates matters because it comes from another word, *bugger,* which means to commit sodomy and is unprintable in England. *Bugger* goes back to Old French *bougre,* a heretic, from Latin *Bulgarus,* a Bulgarian. Bulgarians were accused of heresy, and then the general hatred of heretics led to the application of *buggery* to the crime of bestiality. In America *bugger* has lost much of its literal meaning and, like *bastard,* has become a relatively harmless slang epithet, "a cute little bugger."

bully. Germanic *buole* was a vulgar term for a lover or sweetheart. The word *bully,* which came from it, had the same meaning in the sixteenth century, but referred especially to a male, a good friend or mate. The meaning degenerated, and Francis Grose's *Dictionary of the Vulgar Tongue* (1796) defines a bully as "a cowardly fellow, who gives himself airs of great bravery." A bully was also a pimp in the eighteenth century. Connotations have changed again, and today a bully is most frequently a person who uses strength or power to intimidate weaker persons. As an adjective, however, *bully* means first-rate, splendid, gallant, as in "Bully for you!" In *bully beef, bully* is a different word, from French *bouillir, to boil.*

bus. *Bus* is an example of clipping or abbreviation as a method of creating words. It is a shortening of *omnibus,* like *still* from *distillery, fan* from *fanatic, wig* from *periwig, zoo* from *zoological gardens,* or *mob* from *mobile vulgus. Omnibus* is the dative plural form of Latin *omnis* and means something like for all. It has developed a number of meanings. It can indicate that something has many purposes or provisions, as in a name for a book collecting the works of an author or in an *omnibus bill* in the legislature. Most commonly it is applied to a large motor coach, a bus, presumably because it can carry many passengers. A *busboy* apparently got his name because he does things for others, especially waiters, perhaps for all.

devil. Greek *diabolos* was a name for a slanderer. It was the origin of Anglo-Saxon *teofol* and then of English *devil,* in Jewish and Christian theology the adversary of God, the spirit of evil. The word has, however, developed a wide variety of less serious meanings. Like *hell* it has become a kind of all-purpose intensive; one can be cold as the devil or hot as the devil. It can be applied to persons in a variety of ways. An unfortunate person can be a poor devil, but another can be a lucky devil; a mischievous child may be a little devil. The devil, the vice, was a popular comic character in medieval and Renaissance drama. A whirling sandstorm is a dust devil.

dog. In Anglo-Saxon times the general term for the common domesticated animal we now call a dog was *hund,* like the modern German word. *Hund* specialized in meaning to modern *hound,* to refer to a particular kind of animal. Anglo-Saxon also had the infrequently used word *docga,* probably derived from Old Norse *dugga,* a headstrong or intractable person, and as *hund* specialized, *dog* generalized to refer to a large group of animals. And *dog* developed many figurative meanings. It became a name for a man, sometimes with favorable connotations as in "lucky dog" or "gay dog," but also suggesting a contemptible fellow as in "dirty dog." It became a name for feet. It suggests some kind of unpleasantness in phrases like "go to the dogs" or "dog-tired." Probably from its shape, an andiron is also known as a *firedog.* Activities of dogs are responsible for the verb *to dog* as in "dog one's footsteps." The same Indo-European root that produced *dog* also produced Latin *canis,* dog, the source of English *canine.* The Romans named two constellations *Canis Major* and *Canis Minor* and called Sirius the dog star. *Dog days* are the hot summer days in July and August when the dog star rises and sets with the sun.

doll. *Doll* developed in the sixteenth century as a nickname for *Dorothy,* similar to *Sal* for *Sarah* or *Moll* for *Mary.* It became slang for a female favorite or a mistress; Doll Tearsheet appears in Shakespeare's *II Henry IV.* It became the name for a model of a person used as a toy, but also developed a variety of more general meanings, for an attractive person of either sex or for any female. Apparently from its shape, a stick with a crosspiece used for stirring in laundering clothes became a *dolly.* A frame on wheels used to transport heavy objects is also a dolly.

doughboy. As early as the 1850s a U.S. infantryman was sometimes called a *doughboy.* A doughboy was a boiled dumpling or a small round doughnut. Nobody is sure how it became a nickname for a soldier, but there have been many guesses. One involves the use of *doughboy* early in the Civil War as the name for large globular brass buttons on infantry uniforms. Supposedly the name transferred to the person wearing the uniform. Another theory is that *dough* described the mud that collected on soldiers in the rainy season. A more elaborate theory notes that Spaniards in the Southwest applied *adobe* to army personnel. This shortened to *dobie* and then to *doughboy.* This seems to me more elaborate than convincing.

enchant. Latin *in-* plus *cantare*, to sing, meant to enchant, particularly to mutter words in a magic formula. In early English *enchant* primarily referred to the practice of witchcraft, but by the sixteenth century it had developed less ominous meanings, to charm or delight without any magic spell.

enthrall. The word *thrall* developed from Anglo-Saxon *thræl*, and it can still have its original meaning, a slave or bondman. Combined with the prefix *en-*, in, it became a verb, and to be *enthralled* was not a pleasant experience. The word has shifted from its literal meaning, to be enslaved, and to be enthralled by a book or a song or a person is to be pleased, charmed, or enchanted by it.

feckless. In the late fifteenth century in Scotland, the word *feck* developed, apparently a shortening of *effect*, to mean purpose, intended result, the point of a statement. It never had much currency outside Scotland, but a century later *feckless*, meaning ineffective, futile, irresponsible, feeble, aimless, did become part of English.

gay. *Gay* came into Middle English from Old French *gai*, of unknown origin, and meant full of joy and mirth, lighthearted, as in "The event lifted my spirits, and I became quite gay." In the twentieth century, however, after "the gay nineties" it specialized in slang as a euphemism to refer to homosexuals, especially male, and then became standard for homosexuals of either sex. It is now almost impossible to use it in its earlier sense.

kind. Anglo-Saxon *cynde*, meaning natural, inborn, is behind both *kin* and *kind*, and in the English of Shakespeare's time *kind* usually meant natural. When Hamlet speaks of Claudius as a "treacherous, lecherous, kindless villain," he is calling him unnatural. The shift to meanings like generous, considerate, sympathetic perhaps reflects an optimistic view of what is natural for human beings.

lackadaisical. *Lackadaisical* has nothing to do with daisies or a lack of them. *Alack* was a Middle English variation on *alas*, as an expression of regret. In the seventeenth century it became part of a common phrase expressing grief or surprise, *alack-a-day*, which then became *lackaday*, alas the day. Then in the eighteenth century the word was extended to *lackadaisy*, and *lackadaisical* developed to mean languid, listless, woebegone. Occasional current mispronunciations of the word as "laxadaisical" suggest a tendency to associate the word with *lack*, want or deficiency or failure, as in compounds like *lackluster*. A similar development is *up* plus *a-day*, which became *up-a-daisy* and then *upsy-daisy*, as an expression used in lifting a child.

languish. *Languish* comes from Latin *languere*, to be

weary, and in the eighteenth century *to languish* was a favorite activity of young ladies in love, expressing an air of wistful melancholy. Lydia Languish was the heroine of Sheridan's play *The Rivals*. The word became so attached to sentimental uses that it is hard to use it seriously today.

legendary. *Legend* came into English from French and originally was the name for a story of the life of a saint. It generalized to refer to any entertaining story that became traditional. *Legendary* referred to something or somebody out of traditional lore; Ulysses was a legendary hero. Modern usage has generalized still further, especially in the overused phrase "a legend in his own time," and *legendary* has become a broad term of praise for an athlete or an entertainer.

lewd. Anglo-Saxon *lǣwede* meant unlettered. Over the centuries the word degenerated in a series of meanings. Chaucer used the word in a variety of ways—to mean rude or uncultivated, to mean lay as opposed to clerical, and to mean ignorant. By Shakespeare's time the word had degenerated to mean vicious or wicked and then more specifically to mean lascivious or lustful.

liberal. From Latin *liber*, free, *liberal* originally meant unrestricted, suitable for a freeman. This sense survives in *liberal arts* or *liberal education*. As an adjective the word most often means generous or openhanded. In its political uses and as a noun, however, a variety of associated prejudices make any objective use of the word difficult.

livid. Latin *livere* meant to be black and blue, and *livid* basically describes the discoloration of the skin caused by a bruise. Through use, however, the color described has varied. *Livid* came to be associated with anger and can also mean reddish or flushed: "Her thoughtlessness made him absolutely livid." But it can also mean pallid, deathly pale: "Fear turned his cheeks livid."

loco. The origin of *loco*, as in *locoweed*, is straightforward; English simply adopted Spanish *loco*, meaning insane or crazy, mainly to name the flowering plant poisonous to range animals, producing what is sometimes called "grass staggers." But the word frequently gets mixed up with another *loco*, a combining form derived from Latin *locus*, place. The Latin phrase *loco citato*, abbreviated *loc.cit.*, has been adopted in English to refer in footnotes to a previously cited passage. *Loci-* developed as a prefix meaning from place to place and combined with Latin *motivus*, meaning moving, to produce *locomotive*. And then about 1834 a man named John Marck invented what he advertised as a self-lighting cigar or match and combined *loco* with the Italian or Spanish word for fire to name it *locofoco*, after *locomotive*, interpreted as "self-moving." The new word moved into politics in 1835 in a meeting of the

Democratic Party in Tammany Hall in New York. The party regulars started the meeting, but a new faction of equal-rights antimonopolists entered later and took over the meeting. The regulars were ousted, but they retaliated by turning off the gas as they left. The rebels were prepared; they had brought candles and the new friction matches, locofoco matches. They produced light and made the party nominations. The next day the papers labeled the group the locofocos, and the name stuck. For a few years it was applied to the Democratic Party generally, especially by opponents exploiting the easy association with *loco* meaning crazy.

logrolling. In America when land was being cleared, neighbors often got together to pile up heavy logs for burning. In lumbering, workers cooperated to roll logs into a stream to be transported to a mill. The term *logrolling* extended to any cooperative activity but also referred specifically to political trading for some purpose like getting a controversial bill passed.

lumber. The verb *lumber* comes from Middle English *lomeren*, which comes from Old Norse, apparently meaning to resound or walk heavily. To move heavily or clumsily is to lumber. Perhaps the noun derived from the verb because heavy, awkward items were called lumber, but a more ingenious explanation connects *lumber* with the Italian city of Lombard, established by invaders whom Julius Caesar called *longobardi*, long beards. Lombardy became a center for money lending, and its pawnshops collected various items held for security, which came to be called *lumber*. Today, especially in England, *lumber* refers to a collection of useless stuff, and a *lumber room* contains old furniture and other discarded items. Specialization, mainly in America, makes *lumber* refer to timber sawed into boards or planks.

lumpen. As an adjective *lumpen* has had some twentieth-century popularity to refer specifically to disenfranchised and uprooted individuals or groups that have lost status. It has also generalized to mean ignorantly contented, stupid, boorish. The word is a back formation from *lumpenproletariat*, a phrase originally used by Karl Marx to designate the lowest level of the proletariat—vagrants and criminals and the lower orders of society.

moot. A *moot point* is subject to further discussion, is not settled. The word comes from Anglo-Saxon *mot* or *gemot*, a meeting or assembly. In early English the word was used to describe a meeting of freemen assembled to administer justice or decide on community problems, and it then became associated with courts. It was applied specifically to arguments in a hypothetical case in a law school, as *moot court*.

mug. *Mug,* as a name for a heavy drinking cup, was introduced into English by the sixteenth century, probably from Scandinavia, where the word came from Old Norse. It's interesting especially for one extension of meaning, based on the fact that the cup was often decorated with a picture of a face. So now a person can have an ugly mug, can overact on the stage by mugging, can have a mug shot taken by a police station photographer. This may explain why a rough and uncouth person may be a mug, and a dubious venture may be a mug's game.

pie. The Latin name for a magpie is *pica;* it became *pie* or sometimes *pye* as the English name for the bird. Then the word expanded in a variety of directions. In the sixteenth century, from the bird's alleged propensity for collecting oddments, the word was applied to a miscellany of fruit or meat baked together. This kind of pie, often a delicacy or dessert, got involved in all sorts of metaphorical and slang adaptations. *Sweetie pie* apparently emphasizes the sugary content of some pies, but *lambie pie* has to do with the cuddly qualities of a live lamb, and *pie* seems to be just a general term of affection. In another general extension, *pie* can refer to anything easily accomplished or conquered, "easy as pie," "it's a piece of pie." Or it can refer to any body of assets or holdings—"We just want a piece of the pie"—or to an impractical or impossible proposal: "The candidate offered a pie-in-the-sky solution." *Pie* is sometimes political graft, and anyone caught with his finger in it may be in trouble. The shape of the baked dish produced *pie-shaped*, *pie chart*, and *pie-faced*, or in the American West, *cow pie*, for cattle or buffalo dung, which dries into a cow chip, sometimes used for fuel. *Pie-eyed* may mean surprised, wide-eyed, but since World War I it usually means drunk. A different characteristic of the pie or magpie, its color, leads to a combination with Welsh *bal*, a white spot, especially the blaze on a horse, to produce *piebald*. A piebald mare is varicolored, especially white and black. Still echoing the magpie's affection for a mixture or jumble, *pie*, frequently spelled *pi*, is used for a mixed collection of printing type or as a verb for the dropping of a line of type to create a pie or pi.

plucky. The verb *pluck* developed through Italian from Latin *pilus*, hair, because it referred to pulling off hair, as well as feathers from a chicken or berries from a bush. It referred also to plucking out the innards of an animal in order to prepare the carcass for market, and then as a noun referred to the liver and heart and lights of a sheep or ox, the items plucked out of the carcass. By humorous extension *pluck* then referred to similar parts of a human being and then in a more serious metaphoric extension to courage or spirit associated with the heart. The same kind of metaphor produced *guts* and *gutsy* or *gutty,* which are still considered coarse by some people but are becoming more acceptable as *plucky* and *grit* and euphemisms like *intestinal fortitude* and *stick-to-itiveness* become old-fashioned.

pony. The Latin word for a young animal was *pullus,* which became Old French *poulenet,* a colt, and then Scottish *powny* and English *pony.* Because a pony was something small, it became the name for a small liqueur glass or the amount such a glass would hold. And apparently because it was something to ride or rely on, it became the name for a translation of a foreign language that a student could use, usually dishonestly, to complete an assignment, a crib. Developing in a different direction *pullus* produced French *poule,* hen, and its diminutive, *poulet,* which became English *pullet.* A pony and a chicken have the same linguistic ancestry.

punk. Nobody is quite sure where the word *punk* came from, although there have been interesting guesses about its origin. One theory, related to the early English use of the word to refer to a prostitute, relates it to Dutch *Punkendiek,* the name of a dike in a Netherlands neighborhood notorious for its red-light district. Meanings shifted and the word came to refer to an inexperienced or incompetent person, especially a second-rate hoodlum.

Another theory observes *punk* as an American Indian word for ashes and relates it to the meaning, especially in America, to refer to soft wood used as tinder. This supposedly was something insignificant or worthless and led to the various uses of *punk* to refer to anything inferior. It is also suggested that both general meanings are related to *funk* and *spunk*. The word becomes more specific in some slang uses, like *punk rock,* for a type of loud music accompanied by special effects of dress and movement.

quick. Anglo-Saxon *cwicu,* alive, became English *quick,* which kept the original meaning, as in "the quick and the dead." Today the word has specialized and usually means rapid or prompt or speedy, but the old meaning persists in a few contexts. *Quicksand* seems to be alive when it engulfs a thing or a person; *quicksilver,* or mercury, is living silver from its liquid form; a *quick wine* is effervescent.

sanction. Latin *sancire,* to make sacred, kept much of its meaning as the origin of *sanctuary* or *sanctity* or *sanctify. Sanction,* however, emphasized one aspect of *sancire,* as it came to mean support or approval, a ratification or permission. The word generalized to refer to any formal decree and then specialized again to refer to a decree that may prohibit an action. In contemporary use the word has come to have two almost opposite meanings (compare *literal,* 27, and *virtual,* 34). A sanction may authorize a person or group to hold a meeting or change a rule. A sanction may also be imposed on a person or a nation forbidding certain behavior or forbidding the export of oil.

shambles. In Old English a *shamble* was a stool and then more specifically a table or stall used for the sale of meat and then a meat market. By the sixteenth century the plural form, *shambles,* named a slaughterhouse, and then generalized to refer to any scene of carnage or wholesale slaughter. Its still more general meaning to refer to any scene of disorder or confusion, a mess, developed in the early twentieth century, first in America. For a time in the mid-nineteenth century, *shambles* was used in America to refer to a slave market, but the usage disappeared with the markets.

shimmy. The French word for shirt, *chemise,* was adopted in English as the name for an undergarment for women, like a short loose slip. The garment was sometimes called a shift, and in some dialects was called a shimmy. The 1920s popular dance, involving much wiggling and shaking, apparently got its name from the underwear, popular about the same time. The word generalized to refer to any vibration or wobbling, especially of automobile wheels.

slut. A Middle English word, *slutte* meant mud or a puddle, and may be partly responsible for *slut,* which referred in Middle English to a slovenly, lazy woman, sometimes to a kitchen maid, a drudge. By Shakespeare's time the meaning had shifted, and a slut was not only slovenly but also sexually promiscuous, a tart, a hussy. Touchstone in *As You Like It* comments on Audrey: "To cast away honesty on a foule slut, were to put good meat into an uncleane dish."

stink. *Stink* was an inoffensive word in Old English, but by the sixteenth century it had degenerated to refer only to a bad smell. *Stench* has the same origin and the same unfortunate development, to refer to only an unpleasant smell. *Stink* generalized beyond its association with smells with a variety of meanings. A political deal can stink. A person can be stinking rich or stinking drunk. *Smell*, which replaced *stink* as an inoffensive word, has tended to degenerate, and even *odor* is more likely to be used as a bad odor than a pleasant one. Perfume manufacturers prefer *scent* and *aroma*.

tin. The name for the metal is an Anglo-Saxon word that has retained its basic meaning but has developed many new meanings from its uses and characteristics. The sound made by striking an object made of tin is *tinny*, and so a piano can have a tinny sound and a bad piano can be a *tin pan*. The district in New York where music publishers had their offices and tried out songs, frequently on bad pianos, became tin-pan alley. A person who can't appreciate music has a *tin ear*. An early Ford car was a *tin Lizzie*. A *tin can* was navy talk for a destroyer and later for a depth charge. Partly from the notion that tin might be substituted for more valuable metals, tin became associated with falseness or insignificance or pretension. *Tinhorn,* apparently from the cheap or flashy appearance of tin horns, came to designate a cheap, flashy person. A tinhorn gambler pretends more importance than he merits; a tinhorn dictator is small-time. A *tintype* is a photograph taken on an iron plate, more professionally called a ferrotype. Motion pictures were once called galloping or jumping tintypes. "Not on your tintype" meant "emphatically no" about 1900, like "not on your life." *Tintinnabulation* has nothing to do with tin or tinny sounds and was not, as is sometimes suggested, coined by Poe in his well-known bells poem. It has a straightforward history, descending directly from Latin *tintinnabulum,* little bell.

tucker. The verb *tuck* came from Anglo-Saxon *tucian,* to pull or pluck, and in later uses became associated especially with cloth. It could refer to the dressing or finishing of cloth or to pulling or folding cloth—"She tucked up her skirts"—or to sewing in a fold or tuck in a garment. A *tucker* was originally a person who dressed cloth stretched out on a frame, called a *tenter.* Then a collar made of the cloth was called a *tucker,* named for the person working on the cloth, as in the phrase "bib and tucker." The cloth the tucker dressed was held on the tenter by tenterhooks. A person on tenterhooks is stretched tight. The verb *tuck* generalized to mean to stuff or cram anything into a narrow space, and then more specifically to stuff into one's stomach, to eat; and in Australia *tucker* became slang for food. In the song "Waltzing Matilda" the jolly swagman, a tramp or vagabond, stuffs a jumbuck, a sheep, in his tucker bag. Possibly from the use of *tuck* to refer to drawing up or shortening clothes, the American use to mean tired or exhausted developed, especially in the phrase "all tuckered out."

villain. In feudal England a *villein* was a peasant who cultivated the fields, subject to the lord of the manor. His name derives from Latin *villanus,* a villager, and a villain was originally just a simple or unsophisticated person, a rustic. By a process of pejoration, the connotations of the word *villain* changed, so that now the word designates a perpetrator of wickedness, especially a character in a play important to the plot because of evil motives or actions.

wench. Anglo-Saxon *wencel* simply meant child, and Middle English *wenche* for a child or young woman had no derogatory significance. The word degenerated to refer to a working girl or maidservant and then to a licen-

tious woman or a prostitute. Currently the word has regained at least partial respectability, and is used in slang to
refer to any young woman, especially an attractive one.

world. *Weorold* in Anglo-Saxon was a combination of
wer, man, and *yldo,* age, and the word meant something
like the age of man or a generation. The sense of *the world*
as the earth did not appear in Anglo-Saxon. The word
preserved its earlier sense in some of its general meanings, to refer to any sphere of existence, any wide scene of
life or action—the world to come. And more specific uses
developed—the ancient world, the animal world, the
world of music. The word can refer to individual experience—"His world is narrow." Today the basic sense is
that *world* refers to the earth or the universe.

CHAPTER 10

Coinages and
Spontaneous Combustion

ALTHOUGH RELATIVELY FEW WORDS IN ENGLISH are creations that can be traced to a specific source, their stories are often interesting. Also interesting are the stories of words that seem to have appeared almost spontaneously, perhaps coined by an unknown enthusiast, perhaps invented to imitate a sound or capitalize on some association. *Brunch* appeared about 1900 and was apparently used facetiously in speaking of anyone too late for breakfast who had to combine breakfast and lunch; it can now describe a social event. *Spam* was invented as a trade name for a kind of canned meat, supposedly by combining *sp* of *spiced* with *am* of *ham*. Spam became a staple in World War II diets, especially in the armed forces, and the name generalized to refer to any canned meat, then to acquire various slang uses—for a medal awarded to everybody in a military force, and in *spam can* for a streamlined locomotive used in England. Most recently *spam* has become a name for unwanted or unsolicited material that can appear on an e-mail site. Some words are acronyms—*radar* (radio detecting and ranging) or *scuba* (self-contained underwater breathing apparatus). A few survive from attempts at clever coinages —*cinemactress, guestimate, workaholic, socialite*. The following stories concern words with checkered, sometimes obscure, pasts.

bamboozle. In the early eighteenth century in comments on "the continual Corruption of our English Tongue" Jonathan Swift mentioned *bamboozle* as a recently invented slang term. It meant to deceive or trick or confuse, as it does now. Swift does not speculate about the origin of the word, and most dictionaries comment "origin unknown," a safe decision. But one dictionary's proposal is at least interesting. It traces the word as a cant form going back to *bombast*. *Bombast* comes from Latin *bambax*, cotton, and still has its base meaning, a soft material used for padding. But metaphorically it developed its more common current meaning, to refer to pompous speech or high-sounding but unimportant language—which might be used to bamboozle someone.

bitter end. Proceeding to the bitter end may have an unpleasant taste, but the origin of the phrase has nothing to do with taste. A *bitt* on a ship is a post around which ropes or cables can be wound and held fast. To wind a cable was to *bitter* it. If the anchor cable on a ship played out to the bitter end, as far as it could go, the ship might be in trouble.

blatant. Edmund Spenser coined or adapted the word *blatant* in Book VI of *The Faerie Queene* (1596) as a name for the Blattant Beast, "a monster bred of hellishe race," whose mouth contained a "thousand tongs," with which he could "rage and roar," tongues of cats, dogs, bears, tigers, and also men. The Blattant Beast is evidently related to Thomas Malory's Questing Beast (see *quest*, 31). Spenser may have coined the word from Latin *blatere*, to babble, or English dialect *blate*, to bellow. It kept meanings like those of the dialect word in early uses. Samuel Johnson, in his 1755 dictionary, defined *blatant* as "Bellowing as a calf," and James Sheridan in his 1789 dictionary simply repeated Johnson's entry. Curiously James Barclay's dictionary early in the nineteenth century defines *blatant* as "bellowing like a cat. Seldom used." Current meanings like obvious, showy, obtrusive, gaudy, appeared in the late nineteenth century.

blurb. Gelett Burgess, 1866–1951, is perhaps best known for his quatrain "The Purple Cow"—"I'd rather see than be one." But he also had success as a coiner of words, producing at least three that made their way into the language—*blurb, bromide,* and *goop. Blurb,* for a brief, usually commendatory notice or advertisement, especially of a book, was coined indirectly. Burgess published *Are You a Bromide?* in 1907, and the publisher decided to present copies to everybody at the annual dinner of the booksellers' association. To distinguish the copies from the regular edition, the publisher prepared a special jacket, with a picture Burgess lifted, possibly from a Lydia Pinkham ad, of a sickly sweet young woman. The woman was labeled Miss Belinda Blurb, her name became associated with a flattering book notice, and *blurb* eventually entered the language.

bromide. In his book *Are You a Bromide? or, The Sulphitic Theory,* Gelett Burgess defined a *sulphite* as "a person who does his own thinking, a person who has surprises up his sleeve." A *bromide* was defined as a person who "does his thinking by syndicate, follows the main-traveled roads, goes with the crowd." A bromide was distinguished by his use of such clichés as "I don't know much about art, but I know what I like." *Sulphite* never had much vogue, but *bromide* caught on at once and became established in the language. *Bromide*, of course, existed in the language long before Gelett Burgess, derived from Greek *bromos*, stink, and naming a medicine used as a sedative. Burgess's adaptation of the word to designate a cliché or trite statement alludes to medicinal bromides as sedatives.

cantankerous. A Middle English word, *conteck* meant contention. In the eighteenth century it spawned *cantankerous*, probably as a humorous coinage influenced by words like *rancorous*, to mean ill-tempered, ill-natured, contradictory. In America in the nineteenth century *cantankerosity* was a humorous version of *cantankerousness*.

canter. In the *Canterbury Tales* Geoffrey Chaucer describes the leisurely pace of pilgrims riding to Canterbury to the shrine of Thomas à Becket. Sometime in the eighteenth century the term *Canterbury gallop* was coined, perhaps partly ironically, to describe their gait. This was abbreviated to *canter*, a moderate gait for a horse, sometimes a trot.

copesetic. With various spellings, *copesetic*, good, satisfactory, excellent, has been American slang since early in the twentieth century, apparently most common in the South. It's one of those words, like *O.K.*, that amateur etymologists can't resist. Some twenty years ago William Safire commented on the word in his column and received dozens of letters confidently explaining the word's origin. One of them, suggested by several people, traced the word to Hebrew *kol b'tzedek,* meaning something like all's well and pronounced like *copesetic.* The notion was that Jewish storekeepers in the South might have used the word, which a child like Bill Robinson could have heard and used. And this ties in with the widespread view that Robinson, Bojangles, the tap dancer, coined the term, probably in the 1930s. Although the word was around as early as 1917, Robinson was born in 1878 and could have originated *copesetic.* But the fact that Robinson used the word is not adequate evidence that he invented it. Linguist Stuart Berg Flexner suggests that "it could come from Creole French *coupersetique,*" although in his slang dictionary he comments only, "From the Yiddish." My favorite explanation, with all the earmarks of folk etymology, turns up in a 1930 novel by Jack Lait, *Gangster Girl:* "In the Palmer House, Chicago, there was a big settee, and when the house detective (cop) sat there, he couldn't see the stairs or elevators. Its significance, therefore, was 'The cop's on the settee,'" which meant all was safe. The story was repeated in a 1939 book, *Gamblers Don't Gamble.* A friend of Eric Partridge, editor of slang dictionaries, suggested, not very seriously, that the word means "able to *cope* and anti *septic*." Linguist Fred Cassidy should have the last word on this one. In a letter to Safire he characterizes various suggestions as "hardly authentic etymology" and observes that sometimes the origin of a word is totally unknown.

cop-out. *Cop* appeared in the early eighteenth century as a verb meaning to capture and, a little later, to steal. It apparently comes from Latin *capere* through French *caper*, to catch or seize. *Cop* as a name for a policeman developed from this use in the middle of the nineteenth century; a policeman is a *copper* or capturer. But there are other theories about the origin of the word. One of them is that *cop*, as a shortening of *copper*, refers to the copper buttons once worn on police uniforms. Another is that the word comes from Yiddish *chop*, to grab. But even before *cop* had anything to do with policemen, the phrase *cop-out* had appeared, with various meanings. It was a variant of *cop it hot*, which meant to be scolded or to get into trouble. In the Boer War *cop-out* was slang for dying. In American slang in the late nineteenth century it could refer to courting a girl or sweetheart, as in "Why don't you cop the lady out?" Then the connection with policemen probably influenced the development of more recent meanings: to be arrested or caught in a crime or to plead guilty in a crime. The latter use, of course, is almost the same as *cop a plea*, to plead guilty as a trade for lighter punishment. And this use has generalized beyond criminal proceedings to refer to any kind of confession or inglorious withdrawal from a project.

curmudgeon. The word *curmudgeon* has been in the language since the sixteenth century, and there are various theories about its origin. One is that it comes from *cornmudgin*, a word formed in the sixteenth century by combining *corn* and *mooch*, to hide or pilfer. A cornmudgin was a corn merchant who hoarded corn in order to push its price up. A more scholarly suggestion by Samuel Johnson derives the word from French *coeur mechant*, evil heart. Johnson defines a curmudgeon as a churl, a griper. Modern definitions are somewhat more charitable toward the curmudgeon, though specifying general cantankerousness.

dingbat. *Ding* goes back to Old Norse *dengja*, to hammer, but is also echoic, suggesting the sound of a bell. *Bat* is an Old English word meaning club or cudgel, which had developed a variety of modern applications, especially in sports. A *brickbat* is a piece of brick handy as a comic-strip missile, but also an unfavorable remark or criticism. The combination *dingbat* was used in America in the nineteenth century to mean a contraption or doohickey or gadget, and currently it refers to ornamental pieces of type used for borders or decorations. It may have been influenced by *dingus,* from Dutch *dinges,* with the same meaning. British slang developed *dingbats,* probably independently, from French *dingot. The dingbats* became a name for delirium tremens or madness. *Ding-a-ling* developed in American slang to characterize a silly person, probably someone who hears imaginary bells. All this probably accounts in some way for the development of *dingbat* to refer to a silly person, a ding-a-ling, often a woman.

gamut. Guido d'Arezzo was an Italian musician born near the end of the tenth century. He coined the names for musical notes that we still use, basing them on the beginnings of words in an old Latin hymn:

> *Ut*queant laxis
> *Re*sonare fibris
> *Mi*ra gestorum
> *Fa*mila tuorum
> *Sol*ve polluti
> *La*bii reatum
> *S*ancte *I*ohannes

The scale emerged as *ut, re, mi, fa, sol, la.* Later another term, *gamma,* was introduced for a lower tone; and before *ut* was changed to *do*, it was combined with *gamma* to produce *gamut*. The word came to refer to the entire musical scale and then by extension to the entire range or extent of anything: "She ran the gamut of emotions."

gobbledygook. Most language coinages have short lives, but a few, like *gobbledygook* catch on. In 1944 Congressman Maury Maverick said, "When concrete nouns are replaced by abstractions, simple terms by pseudo-technical jargon, the result is gobbledygook." His coinage is now part of the language.

goop. In the 1930s Gelett Burgess invented some unconventional children who didn't brush their teeth or obey their parents. He called them goops. In America *goop* generalized to refer to any silly or boorish person, a goof. In England a goop is a silly or fatuous person, probably with no relation to the Burgess characters and probably as a variation on *goof*. The slang use of *goop* to mean nonsense or baloney also seems unrelated. *Goop* or *goup* is an expressive coinage like *glop* or *gook* to refer to any viscous, sticky, gooey substance, from dripping chocolate frosting to a gelatin used to clean grease from a garage floor.

hornswoggle. *Hornswoggle,* to cheat or hoax, to get the better of, is an example of the fanciful coinages that came out of the American West early in the nineteenth century. Others, with no clear linguistic origin, include *rambunctious, honeyfuggle, sockdolager, absquatulate, slumgullion.* Often some kind of association with other words may be behind the coinages, but they are seldom clear. *Hornswoggle* may be related to the horns that supposedly sprout on the head of a cuckold. *Rambunctious* has been associated with *rum*, as a cause for boisterous behavior, or with *ram*, as an animal given to unruliness. *Absquatulate*, to leave, depart, may echo *abscond*. *Sockdolager* can define a sock or decisive blow, but by extension it is an exceptional person or thing. *Slumgullion* sounds like something that might be eaten in a slum.

hot dog. *Hot dog* as the name for a frankfurter in a soft bun, usually with mustard, has become an international colloquial term and has inspired a number of stories about its origin, all of them suggesting some kind of canine origin for the wiener. H. L. Mencken records that Harry Mozely Stevens, caterer at the New York Polo Grounds, introduced the frankfurter sandwich sometime after 1900 and credited T. A. Dorgan with coining the name *hot dog*, presumably because of the folk belief that the sausages were made from dog meat. Another popular legend gets more specific about the composition of the wieners. It reports that the wieners were called dachshund sausages and suggests that cartoonist Dorgan didn't know how to spell *dachshund* and took the easy way out by labeling his picture of a barking sandwich simply *hot dog*. A totally different story reports that the hot dog was introduced by Charles Feltman, a Coney Island baker, and there is a record that in 1913 the Coney Island Chamber of Commerce passed a resolution forbidding the use of *hot dog* on signs at Coney Island. There is no evidence on how this resolution is related to Feltman. But *Coney Island* did become a name for a lunch wagon or hot-dog stand and for one kind of large hot dog. By the 1920s *hot dog!* had become a slang exclamation denoting elation or surprise or approval, even expanding to *hot diggety dog*. More recently a hot dog is a show-off, especially in athletics.

hunky-dory. In some parts of America in the nineteenth century *hunk*, from Dutch *honk*, meaning a station or goal, was used in games like tag for a goal or home. It generalized as slang to refer to a safe place or anything safe or good. Mark Twain observed, "We're all hunky, after all." It extended to *hunky-dory*, all right. Another *hunk*, probably of Dutch origin, named a chunk cut from a cheese or a loaf, and then by extension came to refer colloquially to a solidly built, muscular, handsome man. As a further complication, *bohunk* and *hunky* developed in American slang, apparently from *Bohemian* and *Hungar-*

ian, as derogatory terms for an immigrant from central Europe. And *hunker* came into English meaning to squat; then with *down* added, to knuckle down, get down to business. Hunkers are what one hunkers on, one's haunches or hams.

jive. One dictionary guesses that *jive* is a coinage after *jibe,* but the connection doesn't seem clear. *Jibe* or *gybe* comes from Dutch *gijpen,* originally to gasp for air, and became a nautical term for swinging sails and then for changing a ship's course. This apparently led to *jibe,* usually with *with,* as a verb meaning to be in harmony with, to be compatible with. *Jive* and *jibe* are sometimes confused, but both seem to me of uncertain origin. *Jive* has developed a variety of uses, mostly slang, as empty, misleading, or pretentious talk or anything false or worthless or jazz or jazz talk or marijuana.

kowtow. English borrowed *kowtow,* also spelled *kotow,* from the Chinese in the early nineteenth century. The Chinese *k'ot'ou* meant to knock the head and referred to the ancient custom of touching the ground with one's forehead when worshiping or showing respect to a distinguished person. The word now usually refers to acting in an obsequious manner.

mugwump. The Algonquian word *mugquomp,* meaning a chief, was picked up in American English in the early nineteenth century to refer to an important man, especially to refer ironically to a self-important man. It became popular as a political term in the 1884 election when it was used to refer to any Republican who refused to support the party candidate, James G. Blaine. Today it has generalized to refer to any person who doesn't take sides, especially a chronic complainer. A popular quip defines a mugwump as a fence-sitter, with his mug on one side and his wump on the other.

pandemonium. Modern society seems to find frequent uses of *pandemonium* to describe scenes of confusion or disorder, from a New Year's Eve celebration to a disastrous fire or bombing. The word originated, however, with a much more specific meaning as one of the relatively few literary coinages that have stayed in the language. John Milton invented the word as the name for the capital of Hell in *Paradise Lost*. He combined Greek *daimon*, demon, with the prefix *pan-*, meaning all or universal, to name Satan's building, populated by all the fallen angels or devils. The word was adopted and generalized.

pumpernickel. The ultimate origin of the name for the dark German bread is obscure, but the word comes from German, where it formerly designated a booby or lout or blockish fellow, and the assumption is that the bread is similarly coarse and heavy. German *pumpen* is to take a heavy fall, and *pumpern* is to break wind. Combined with *nickel*, a goblin, both have been proposed as the source of *pumpernickel* to name a dull fellow. *Nickel* is from the name *Nicholas*, which was *Nikolaos* in Greek, a combination of *nike*, victory, and *laos*, the people. *Nick*, usually *Old Nick*, became a name for Satan or the Devil. A similar relationship is behind another nickname for the devil, *Old Scratch*. It is a variant of Old English *scrat*, a goblin or monster.

quiz. Various anecdotes have been cited to explain the origin of *quiz*. For example, there is the story that a Dublin theater manager named Daly bet that he could create a new word without meaning that would stay in the language. He supposedly chalked the letters Q-U-I-Z on walls all over the city. People were puzzled and asked "What?" which gave the letters a meaning. The tale is an obvious example of folk etymology. Dictionaries agree that the origin of *quiz*, which appeared in the middle of the nineteenth century, is unknown, although some suggest a possible association with Latin *quis*, who or what.

scalawag. A small horse from Shetland was known as a *sheltie*, but small ponies and cattle imported from Shetland were also *scalloways*, from Scalloway, formerly the capital of Shetland. The word became *scalawag* and was easily extended to refer to any small worthless animal and then any worthless person. To complicate the etymology, there is a dialect word, *scallag*, used in the Hebrides for a poor tenant who works five days a week for a master and then is allowed on the sixth to cultivate a little land for himself. In America by the middle of the nineteenth century, *scalawag* was in use to refer generally to a scamp or loafer or rascal or to a worthless animal, as in *scalawag steer*. The word also developed a specific use during the Reconstruction period after the Civil War. It was applied by opponents to Southerners who supported the Republican Party. Northerners who were Republicans in the South were carpetbaggers.

serendipity. *Serendipity* is a literary coinage that has acquired popularity as a pseudolearned word for a general state of well-being. In the eighteenth century Horace Walpole wrote a fairy tale called "The Three Princes of Serendip." Serendip was an early name for Ceylon, now Sri Lanka. In a letter to a friend, Walpole said that he had invented *serendipity* to designate a special skill of the three princes, a faculty for accidentally making happy discoveries. There did not seem to be a great demand for a name for this specific faculty, but the word persisted and generalized to its current vague sense.

sirloin. In a manor house, Hoghton Tower, near Preston in western England, there is a brass plaque on one wall on which is written an account of a visit to the manor in the early seventeenth century of the English king and his retinue. According to the plaque, the king admired the beef served in his honor and dubbed it "Sir Loin." The story on the plaque repeats an old legend and indicates that a British king in the seventeenth century had the same faith in folk etymology as current owners of restaurants named "Sir Loin's." Actually the word comes from French *sur*, above, and *longe*, loin, and came into English long before the visit to Hoghton Tower simply to locate the cut of meat.

skedaddle. J. F. Hotten's dictionary of slang, published about the time the word *skedaddle* became popular in the middle of the nineteenth century, says confidently, "The word is very fair Greek, the root being that of *skedammuni*, to 'retire tumultuously,' and it was probably set afloat by some professor at Harvard." There is not much evidence to support this derivation, but the word was in use in the nineteenth century in some English dialects, meaning to spill or scatter, especially in "skedaddle the milk." It turned up in America during the Civil War meaning to leave hastily and reached a peak of popularity early in the twentieth century, to be replaced by terms like *skiddoo, scram,* and *absquatulate.*

skulduggery. *Skulduggery* has nothing to do with skulls or digging, but developed as an Americanism in the nineteenth century, apparently as a variation on Scottish *skulduddery,* meaning fornication or obscenity. The American adaptation softened the meaning to trickery or craftiness.

slumgullion. American slang developed the word *slumgullion* in the nineteenth century, and it acquired a variety of meanings. In hobo use, which may have been the earliest, it described any meat or vegetable stew; or it could refer to a cheap, watery drink. In mining it was used to refer to the refuse or mud of sluice boxes, and whalers used it to designate the blood and oil that dripped from blubber. These uses were adapted to provide a name for a low, worthless fellow. The word may come from *salmagundi,* which has a respectable scholarly history, going back to Latin *sal* for salt and *condire,* to pickle. Old French *salmagondin* was a name for seasoned salt meats. Another theory derives *slumgullion* from *slubberdegullion,* which appeared in the seventeenth century as a name for a slobbering or dirty fellow, a worthless sloven. *Slubberdegullion* apparently combined *slobber,* to dribble from the mouth, with *gullion,* a variation on a Latin word for testicle.

tantrum. *Tantara* developed in the sixteenth century to name a sound it imitated, the blare of a trumpet, a fanfare. *Tantrum*, originally *tantarum*, may be a pseudo-Latin coinage from *tantara*, to designate a fit of temper or outburst of rage that sometimes sounds like the blare of a trumpet. *Doldrums* for a state of low spirits or listlessness may have been formed from *dull* to describe the opposite of *tantrum*. *Doldrums* now refers especially to equatorial regions of the ocean noted for dead calms.

utopia. Sir Thomas More named his 1516 description of an imaginary ideal society *Utopia*, creating the word from Greek *ou*, not, and *topos*, place, suggesting that the ideal society exists nowhere. As a common noun the word now refers to any ideal imaginary place or political system, but the ironic implications of More's title remain. In the late nineteenth century, indeed, two utopias had the same kind of title, Samuel Butler's *Erewhon*, *nowhere* spelled backward, and William Morris's *News from Nowhere*. A recent variation is the creation of the term *dystopia*, using the prefix *dys-*, bad or ill, to name an imaginary society in which technological progress has resulted in a degradation of values or quality of life.

vaseline. Robert A. Chesebrough coined *vaseline* as a trade name in the late nineteenth century from German *wasser*, water, and Greek *elaion,* oil. It continues as a trademark but has also become a common noun in English and several other languages. *Kodak* was coined by George Eastman in 1888, also as a trade name. The word derives partly from Eastman's mother's name, which began with *k.* It also has became a widely used common noun.

INDEX